Loss and
Social Work

Transforming Social Work Practice – titles in the series

To order, please contact our distributor: BEBC Distribution, Albion Close, Parkstone, Poole, BH12 3LL. Telephone: 0845 230 9000, email: **learningmatters@bebc.co.uk**. You can also find more information on each of these titles and our other learning resources at www.learningmatters.co.uk.

Loss and Social Work

CAROLINE CURRER

Series Editors: Jonathan Parker and Greta Bradley

LearningMatters

First published in 2007 by Learning Matters Ltd.
Reprinted in 2008

British Library Cataloguing in Publication Data
A CIP record for this book is available from the British Library.

ISBN-13: 978 1 84445 088 6

The right of Caroline Currer to be identified as the Author of this Work has been asserted by her in accordance with the Copyright, Designs and Patents Act 1988.

Cover and text design by Code 5 Design Associates Ltd
Project management by Deer Park Productions
Typeset by Pantek Arts Ltd, Maidstone, Kent
Printed and bound in Great Britain by Bell & Bain Ltd, Glasgow

Learning Matters Ltd
33 Southernhay East
Exeter EX1 1NX
Tel: 01392 215560
info@learningmatters.co.uk
www.learningmatters.co.uk

Contents

Acknowledgements

This book owes its existence to the cohorts of social work students who have laughed, cried and shared their experiences of loss with me; as well as to those people who have supported me whilst writing, especially my husband Alan. My thanks also go to Carol Holloway and Mary Pennock who have, at different times, co-led the 'Loss and Social Work' module with me, bringing their own distinctive experience, insights and wisdom to our work together. In particular, the use of the concept of 'cradling' in relation to resilience (see Chapter 4) was suggested by Mary.

Introduction

Whether you are a student social worker, or have been qualified for many years, this book has relevance for your practice. Loss is a key aspect of social work, and the grief that service users and carers experience – sometimes even related to social work intervention – cannot and should not be ignored by those working with them. Yet the subject is one that is often not given the attention it merits within social work education and training (Thompson, 2002a, Goldsworthy, 2005).

This book has been written for student social workers undertaking qualifying training at undergraduate level. Yet I hope that it will also meet the needs of students on postgraduate programmes as well as those undertaking post-qualifying training, and of social workers who seek to update their knowledge and skills outside the framework of formal courses. Theory and research relating to loss and grieving have changed and developed greatly in recent years, to the extent that one leading writer (Walter, 1996) has described this as a 'revolution' in the ways in which we understand loss and grief. By seeking to outline these developments, I hope that there will be plenty here of interest to those currently in social work practice who qualified some years ago. Those considering a career in social work, or who work alongside social workers, should also be able to apply the insights to their own practice and experience.

Requirements for social work education

Social work was defined in 2001 by the International Association of Schools of Social Work and International Federation of Social Workers as follows:

> The social work profession promotes social change, problem solving in human relationships and the empowerment and liberation of people to enhance well-being. Utilising theories of human behaviour and social systems, social work intervenes at the points where people interact with their environments. Principles of human rights and social justice are fundamental to social work. (Joint agreed definition, 27 June 2002, Copenhagen)

Theories of loss and grieving are amongst the theories of human behaviour that need to be used by social workers. Change is – by this definition – at the heart of the social work task, yet it is also, in a different sense, at the heart of the experience of many service users. Loss involves change – it results from it and leads to it. Such change is frequently unwanted, and the problems that service users face often involve wrestling with how to make sense of, and live with, loss and change. Empowerment and liberation can lie in finding positive ways to work with unwelcome changes, and it is often very humbling to witness the courageous ways in which people do this. Whatever our area of practice, social work involves standing alongside service users and being involved with them as they engage in solving the problem of how to survive and go forward in the midst of loss and change. This book explores the ways in which a knowledge of the processes involved in grieving and responding to loss may be used to help those with whom we work who are faced with such challenges.

Social work education in the UK has undergone a major transformation to ensure that qualified social workers are educated to honours degree level and that they develop knowledge, skills and values which are common and shared. We are now seeing the third cohort of graduates from the initial degree level programmes. Registration of both qualified and student social workers has given the social work profession a means by which fitness to practise can be monitored – both in terms of meeting educational requirements, and in relation to conduct. In common with others in the series, this book uses the National Occupational Standards for social work and the Quality Assurance Agency's benchmark criteria for social work as a means to show how the content of each chapter fits into the requirements for qualifying training. For student social workers, courses are arranged in different ways, with modules covering different aspects of the curriculum. Loss may be a theme running through several modules or course units or it may – although this is less likely – be a course in its own right. Whatever the structure of the programme, knowledge of loss and grief has a place within it.

The book's structure

This book has five main chapters. The first emphasises that loss and change are aspects of life experience for all of us, not just for service users, and looks at the implications that this has for you as a social worker. It considers the importance of the topic in terms of both policy and practice. You will be invited to identify both the losses that service users experience within a setting of interest to you (perhaps your placement or area of work) as well as your own losses and the impact that they have had. We look at research into what service users expect of social workers and find that these include the ability to engage in relationships that involve the self – something that is only possible if you are able to be self-aware and comfortable with using your own experience in ways that are appropriate. This chapter introduces the terms that we will be using and identifies dimensions and themes that will recur throughout the book. By the end of the chapter, you should have more knowledge about issues of loss and change and their place in social work practice. As well as this, the chapter will also help you to identify a number of questions. For example, is loss mainly a cognitive or an emotional matter? What can we hope for following a major loss or crisis – do we look to 'recover', to endure or perhaps to grow through an experience of loss? What is the balance in working with those experiencing loss between focusing on the future and on the past? These and other questions will be explored in further chapters.

The second chapter focuses upon social and cultural aspects of loss and grief. This counteracts a tendency to see loss as a very individual experience, and the chapter argues that this tendency is a feature of the ways in which society and culture define the focus of academic study, as well as everyday life. The social focus found in this chapter is important because it links with the social work commitment to anti-oppressive practice. The chapter draws upon cross cultural research to look at the ways in which loss and grief are socially defined and moulded. You will also look at social customs and rituals and how these define and regulate behaviour as well as offering support at times of loss.

Chapter 3 introduces and discusses theoretical models of grieving, reviewing both earlier and more recent theories. You will be introduced to these in relation to their research base, and also invited to explore how they relate to your own experience. Key themes and issues are identified, as well as the underlying theoretical perspectives, and the chapter ends by identifying implications for practice.

Throughout the book, you will become aware that much of the research base relates to loss through death. Yet bereavement is only one type of loss, and many of the situations that we meet as social workers involve other losses. In all of the chapters, you will therefore be challenged to consider how the points made relate to a broad spectrum of losses. This is particularly so in Chapter 4, which asks you to focus upon the links between theory and practice by critically examining the application of models to work with children and with older adults. What, if any, differences are there? This chapter outlines a number of 'determinants of grief' and invites you to explore a situation of loss other than death while using these as a framework. The situation you choose may be one that arises from a placement, from your work or from personal experience – it is up to you. The important thing here is to get used to using theoretical perspectives in a flexible way to help you to understand different situations. This chapter also looks at the concept of resilience, and at what has been called 'ambiguous loss'. It ends by considering how we can both use and abuse theories and models.

The final chapter considers the social work response. Responding in situations of loss and grief is often thought of in terms of 'counselling', but this chapter looks at a range of other responses. Firmly rooted in the importance of multi-disciplinary work, the chapter also explores the social work role, and asks you to identify ways in which social workers may deny grief or fail to respond, and the reasons for this. This will bring you back to the use of self, and the need for good supervision as well as support in terms both of structures and of relationships if you are to be enabled to respond appropriately to the grief of service users.

Learning features

An important aspect of this book is that it is interactive. Activities invite you to draw upon your existing knowledge and experience, to test out the ideas outlined as you go through the chapters, to apply them to practice and to explore your own responses. You will look at your own learning needs and at your own past experience. Case studies also help you to see how the issues work out in practice, and research summaries seek to offer short overviews of relevant material. Loss is not a subject that can be approached impersonally or theoretically – the issues raised are likely to strike a chord, maybe even touch a nerve – and so these activities are an important part of your learning. They should help you to integrate knowledge as you go through the book, and perhaps even stimulate disagreement or alternative perspectives.

A 'health warning'

This brings me to an important 'health warning'. Loss is an emotive subject, and even studying it, reading reports of research and considering case examples can trigger emotions and thoughts associated with our own experiences. When I am teaching this subject, I ask students to identify a 'buddy' within the class with whom they can discuss any reactions or personal issues that have been raised by the material from each session. A book presents a different challenge, because I cannot judge the effect that reading this book may have on you, or ensure that you have adequate personal support as you think about these issues. You may wish to consider how to arrange this for yourself. It can be useful to keep a note-book or journal and make a note of the responses that you have to the activities that are part of this book. This has two purposes – it provides a way to 'offload', but it also gives you a chance to look back and reflect on your own learning and responses. In this area, more perhaps than any other, you need to develop some habits that will be useful when you encounter these issues in the practice setting. It is because I know that you will encounter them in your practice that I make no apology for raising them here – better to explore your own experience in the comparative 'safety' of a library or your place of study than when you are in the company of a service user who needs your undivided attention.

Professional development and reflective practice

This book is all about your development as a reflective practitioner and it is my hope that it will offer you a means to deepen your own experience in this respect. It is one of the requirements within the Codes of Practice for social care workers that we engage in ongoing professional development. If you are already qualified, working through this book might even be an activity undertaken as part of your application for ongoing professional registration. Whatever your situation, reflection upon loss and grief is not a 'once and for all' activity, but something that we all need to do on a regular basis.

Chapter 1
Loss and grief in social work

A C H I E V I N G   A   S O C I A L   W O R K   D E G R E E

This chapter will help you begin to meet the following National Occupational Standards.
Key Role 1: Prepare for, and work with individuals, families, carers, groups and communities to assess their needs and circumstances.
2.3 Work with individuals, families, carers, groups and communities to enable them to analyse, identify, clarify and express their strengths, expectations and limitations.
Key Role 2: Plan, carry out, review and evaluate social work practice, with individuals, families, carers, groups, communities and other professionals.
5.3 Apply and justify social work methods and models used to achieve change and development, and improve life opportunities.
Key Role 5: Manage and be accountable, with supervision and support, for your own social work practice within your organisation.
14.4 Use professional and managerial supervision and support to improve your practice.
Key Role 6: Demonstrate professional competence in social work practice.
19.4 Critically reflect upon your own practice and performance using supervision and support systems.

It will also introduce you to the following academic standards as set out in the social work subject benchmark statement.
3.1.4 Social work theory.
• Social science theories explaining group and organisational behaviour, adaptation and change.
3.1.5 The nature of social work practice.
• The processes of reflection and evaluation, including familiarity with the range of approaches for evaluating welfare outcomes, and their significance for the development of practice and the practitioner.
3.2.2 Problem solving skills.
• Manage the processes of change.
3.2.5 Skills in Personal and Professional Development.
• Advance their own learning and understanding with a degree of independence;
• Reflect on and modify their behaviour in the light of experience;
• Identify and keep under review their own personal and professional boundaries;
• Manage uncertainty, change and stress in work situations.

Introduction

Loss is an everyday experience. Yet the fact that we all experience loss does not mean that we know all about it or that the experience of loss is uniform. This chapter therefore starts by looking at ways in which the experience of loss is both common and variable. You will probably not be surprised when I say that I think that this topic is one that is particularly important for you as a social worker – in the second section of this chapter I hope to convince you that this is the case.

Since loss is a term that we often use in ordinary conversation, and something that we all experience, we must also start this book by defining the words that we use. When an experience is familiar, it is easy to assume that we know what is meant by common words. If we are to study this topic in more depth, we must be precise in our use of language. For example, does the word 'grief' refer only to the sadness following a death, or can it apply to a broader range of situations? Is it about the way we feel, or about the way we think about ourselves? These questions will be looked at more deeply in Chapter 3, but definitions and some initial distinctions form the third part of this first chapter.

Because loss is a common experience you start with an advantage, namely that you already know quite a bit about the issues that we will be discussing in this book. I can say this with confidence, even though I do not know anything about you – your gender, age or racial background, for example. Later in this chapter, I will say more about the use we can make of our own experience, and the dangers that this can pose for us as social work practitioners, but for now I just want to underline the fact that loss is a normal part of life for all of us. This may seem obvious, but it is an aspect of this particular subject that is crucially important – both for you as a social worker and for you as you read this book. The activities will ask you to draw on your own experience. Used well by a sensitive, reflective and well-supported practitioner, our own experience of loss and grief has the potential to enhance our practice in ways that we will explore further throughout this book.

Commonalities and variations in relation to loss

Although it is true to say that we all experience loss as part of our lives, it is also clear that not everyone experiences the same amount of loss. In addition, all of us do not perceive situations in the same way. Thus some may see a situation as a loss whilst others do not. We can in turn also observe differences in the ways in which we express loss and in our response to it. Some people seem to become stronger following a loss, whilst others are crushed by it. We start by considering the ways in which economic and social factors contribute to the amount of loss that we experience.

Variations in the extent and impact of loss

Tragedies affecting those who are rich and powerful sell newspapers: perhaps it is comforting to know that those who are materially rich also experience loss. Yet whilst money and economic security are no guarantee of long life or of happiness in individual cases, they can protect people from loss, and from what are known as 'secondary losses'. Let us first use the example of death – the loss of life itself. Proverbs in a variety of languages proclaim that *death is the great leveler*, and it is certainly true that we will all die, and that awareness of this fact can make social differences appear trivial. Yet the idea of equality in relation to death and dying is illusory. If we look at the social patterning of death in a world perspective, we can see that those who live in poorer countries die younger. In the UK also those in lower social classes have a shorter life expectancy. In all these figures, there are also gender differences.

RESEARCH SUMMARY

In England and Wales, class differences in life expectancy have risen. Using the Registrar General's Social Class system, based on occupation, statistics show a difference of five years in life expectancy for a male child born into the higher social classes compared to a male child born into the lower classes. For female babies the difference is three years. Between 1972 and 1996, there was a rise of about a year in the differential. This means that whilst there is rising life expectancy overall, the class differentials for both men and women are becoming more marked. The probability of surviving to over 85 years is notably higher for those who have been in non-manual rather than manual occupations. (Source: Hattersley, 1999)

If we look at world statistics, we see that in 2000, a child born in Afghanistan had a life expectancy of 42 years, whilst one born the same year in the UK had a life expectancy of 77 years – a difference in life expectancy at birth of 35 years. (Source: **www.un.org/esa/ population/publications/long-range_working-paper_final.pdf**)

The implications of a loss: secondary losses

What is true in terms of the ultimate loss of life is also true for other situations of loss, and for the consequences of a major loss. Consider the loss of sight as experienced by Mary and Joan in the scenario below.

CASE STUDY

Mary Taylor and Joan Simms meet in the ophthalmic outpatients department of their local hospital. Both are white, in their early seventies and retired – Mary from a high powered executive job in London, and Joan from a cleaning job in a local shop. Mary has a good occupational pension; Joan relies on state benefits. Neither has children, and both live alone, but they are each house-proud and live close to friends who they see frequently. Both see themselves as happy and resourceful. It has been an enormous shock for both of them to find that they are losing their sight.

Mary can afford to pay for substantial alterations to be made to her home. She is able to remain there and to increase the help that she already has with the housework. Now that she can no longer drive, she has made an arrangement with a local taxi firm to be taken out when her friends are unable to help out so that she retains some independence.

Despite an assessment of her needs that leads to some additional benefits and specialist resources, Joan's council house cannot be adapted sufficiently to enable her to remain there safely. She is re-housed in an area that is not very far away but has a poor bus service. Since she and her friends are reliant on public transport, the strong practical support that she once enjoyed dwindles to infrequent telephone contact. She becomes reluctant to go out.

This shows that the implications of a loss vary, and that financial security, together with other factors such as social support, can affect the implications of a loss for individuals, and can also protect people from what are known as secondary losses – losses that result directly from another, primary, loss. Losing your sight is a serious loss for anyone, but not everyone loses their house or their friends as a result.

Variations in the way that loss is perceived

There are variations too in the way that losses are perceived. There are even some situations that one person may see as loss, and another may see as gain. Take the example of redundancy.

CASE STUDY

A local packing firm closes, and over 100 people are made redundant. Tom, Frank and John used to work together. Tom has four children and is the sole breadwinner. He has worked in this place for over 20 years, and his family are dependent on the money he brings in, but together with his partner the couple have a strong social network which focuses on the children and the parents of their school friends.

John has also worked for the firm for many years; he is divorced and sees his children on alternate weekends – his financial outgoings are less, but this job was the only thing that kept him going when his wife left him for another man. Since his divorce, he has few friends outside work.

Frank has a partner and one child; his partner has a good job. He has been frustrated with this job for some time and dreams of re-training and setting up his own business.

Although redundancy affects many people, and has the same implications in terms of the wages and work time that are gone, it will be experienced very differently by those involved. Individual financial and social circumstances play a part in this – was that wage essential for a family, and was work the centre of a person's social life? We can see that there are different implications for Tom and for John in these respects. Less tangible factors also come into play, such as the meaning of work for the person made redundant. For some, perhaps like John, the wage itself may not be as important as being seen by others and/or themselves as a 'breadwinner'. The case study also shows, through Frank's circumstances, that not everyone feels the same way about their work. A loss may become an opportunity – a chance, in this instance, to pursue the dream of setting up his own business.

What can we learn from this example? We need to distinguish what is gone or taken away from both its practical implications and its significance for the individual concerned. There is a social dimension to this also. Not only does the loss have meaning for the individual concerned, it has meanings for those around them, and these meanings may well not be the same. Thus, work may be part of John's self-image but less important for his children's view of him, except insofar as it affects his available time or finances.

Variations in the way we express and respond to loss

So far, I have looked at how loss may be experienced. We also need to consider how it is expressed. Because expression is a form of communication with other people, it is governed by social norms. Take the familiar (although I hope now not universally accepted) saying that *big boys don't cry*. Whatever individual differences there are in what we feel, there are powerful – and often unstated – social expectations concerning how we express our feelings in situations of loss. In Chapter 2, we will be looking more closely at the whole area of social expectations, and the way that grief is regulated and even 'policed' in society – our social and cultural context influences how we speak and act, how we ask for help (or not) and also how others respond to us.

Resilience and the themes of coherence and control

Why is it that some people are devastated by loss, whilst others seem to experience a large amount of tragedy and loss and seem to survive better, and even to grow stronger as a result? The subject of resilience is an important one, and has attracted increased attention in recent years. We need to bear it in mind throughout this book. Some early work on this (Antonovsky, 1987) identified two factors that will be useful in our ongoing discussion of loss. These are control and coherence.

Our discussion has already introduced these two themes. In looking at economic factors and their importance, we have acknowledged that the ability to control our environment has an impact in terms of protection from secondary loss, and softening the blow of an initial loss itself. And in considering the importance of the way that losses are perceived, both by the person themselves and by others around them, we have touched on the theme of coherence, which refers to the meaning that a situation has for the person concerned. Watch out for these two themes as we go through the book. As a starting point, it is not a bad thing to begin to ask the following two questions about any loss:

- What does this mean for the person I am with, and for those around them?

- What (if any) control do they have over what is happening and its effects?

There are two aspects to the second question: the control that a person actually has, and the control that they see themselves as having. For example, Joan's financial situation gave her less control over her life than Mary. Yet her sense of loss also led to the feeling that she was totally helpless and that her loss had destroyed her life. A person with a different outlook might still have believed in their own ability to be in control. This will be an important distinction when we consider the theme of resilience in Chapter 4.

Why is loss an important topic for social workers?

There are a number of reasons why loss is an important topic for social workers. Firstly, the themes of loss, change and transition feature in the social policies that underpin social work practice. Secondly, social workers typically intervene at times of crisis – and hence of loss – in peoples' lives. Thirdly, we know that service users want social workers who are able to relate to them as human beings, and who are therefore familiar with and able to acknowledge pain and loss in their own lives as well as those of service users. Despite this, we also know that social work training often pays little attention to loss as a core theme or subject. I will look at these points in turn.

Change, transition and loss as factors in policy

This is apparent from the extracts from the National Occupational Standards and Benchmark Statement that are shown at the start of each chapter in this book, but also in some legislation and other policy documents. In relation to the care of children, for example, *supporting transitions* is one of the six headings within the Common Core that underpins recent changes and legislation. This focuses on the everyday changes that accompany growing up but it is also noted that there are other particular transitions that are faced by some children, such as *family illness or the death of a close relative; divorce and family break-up; issues related to sexuality; adoption; the process of asylum; disability; parental mental health; and the consequences of crime* (DfES, 2005: 16). It is suggested that everyone working with children needs to *know about the likely impact of key transitions, such as divorce, bereavement, family break-up, puberty, move from primary to secondary school, unemployment and leaving home or care* (DfES, 2005: 17), in the context of understanding how children and young people respond to change.

The National Service Framework for Mental Health (DoH, 1999) mentions divorce and unemployment – both situations involving significant losses – as being linked with increased vulnerability to mental illness.

In services for older people, a link with loss and change is not explicit in policy documents. Recent publications on implementing the national service framework for older people (see for example DoH, 2006) focus on the importance of promoting independence, dignity and choice. The responsiveness of services is rightly seen as an important factor. It is interesting that although one of the key programmes relates to spreading best practice in relation to services for dying people to meet the needs of non-cancer patients (which includes many people dying in old age), loss and grief are not mentioned in this document. An upbeat introduction focusing on the benefits of old age is perhaps a welcome corrective to the previous use of ageist terms such as 'burden' to describe our ageing population. I would suggest, however, that we need to beware of a swing to the other extreme where the very real losses that accompany ageing are denied in the interests of the current emphasis on choice and independence. Those working with older people – as well as those working with children – need to be aware of issues of loss and grief if they are to practise effectively. This issue is discussed further in Chapter 4.

Intervening at times of crisis

Although social workers work in widely differing settings, with people of different ages and circumstances, it is probably true to say that social workers usually become involved at a time of crisis in someone's life. Of course, in some settings a social worker may continue to work with a person or family when a crisis has passed, and some people will have ongoing involvement with a social worker. A crisis is a time of change, and frequently those that result in social work involvement are neither planned nor positive for the people involved. So although everyone experiences loss at some time, and although not all losses result in a need for social work services, those situations that do give rise to social work intervention usually involve loss as a key dimension.

Take a look at the following quotation:

> *Without an understanding of loss and related issues, practitioners in the human services can be seen to be at a distinct disadvantage in terms of making sense of the complex situations encountered, as loss and grief are such pervasive and influential factors in human behaviour and interactions.* (Thompson, 2002a, p1)

Now think about how this applies in the area of practice most familiar to you – or pick an area of social work practice that interests you.

ACTIVITY 1.1

Think of and specify an area of social work practice. List the losses that service users commonly experience, starting with those that bring them into contact with the service, and then list any other losses that may be part of the same picture.

Comment

Very often becoming a user of social work services itself involves the loss of some degree of self-esteem or independence. Depending on the area of practice you have chosen, you may also have listed the loss of a home or neighbourhood, or perhaps a loss of freedom, or a school, or work, friends, parents or children. Some losses concern particular people or relationships. Some are about places or familiar surroundings. Some are less tangible or obvious, such as those concerning freedom, independence or self-esteem. Some then become losses at the level of self-perception – because there is a loss of independence, a person may come to see themselves as having little control over life generally; because one relationship is lost, they may come to see themselves as someone who cannot relate to other people; because a particular environment or place is lost, a person may lose their confidence to go out. In this way, loss can be a complex and escalating experience, not just in terms of the secondary losses that follow in a practical way, but through the impact on a person's own self-perception and the way they are treated by other people. The initial loss may become, over time, less important than what follows on from it.

It is worthwhile remembering here that loss can accompany changes that are – on the face of it – positive. You can probably recognise situations in your own life that you have chosen but which have brought loss. For example, marriage or a new relationship can bring significant pleasure and gain but also involve a loss of freedom and independence. Similarly, someone may take on a new job or move to a new house and wonder why they are spending so much time feeling sad about what has been left behind. It is particularly important to remember this when working with service users. Frequently a social worker will work hard to bring about a change that improves life for the service user. Then instead of looking at the benefits, the service user focuses on what has been left or lost. Can you think of such an example from your own practice?

Differing perceptions of the same situation

To make matters more complicated, we are often not working with just one individual but instead with a family or a group of people, who may all perceive a situation differently and also focus on different aspects. Consider the following example:

CASE STUDY

A woman of 88 years moves into residential care following a fall at home. Her daughter, who lives at a distance, is pleased that at last her mother will be cared for – she had been increasingly worried about her safety. The woman herself has mixed feelings, but her overriding emotion is of sadness at leaving the home in which she lived for over 50 years. On the other hand, she had been finding the housework too much, and is relieved that she will no longer have this to do.

Her neighbour (also in her late eighties) is very distressed – they have been close friends and the residential home is too far for her to visit regularly. They used to see each other daily for coffee.

This example reminds us that we must check out how the situation is perceived by all of those involved. In some situations a social worker will be working with all the members of a family; in other situations the focus of work will be with a particular individual and their experience will be the most important. But knowing how others around them see the situation will still be important to help both the social worker and the service user to appreciate the wider picture, and perhaps why others are responding in an unexpected way.

What service users look for from social workers

So what do we know about the things that service users appreciate from the social workers who work with them? Evidence from two recently published books paints a picture that is remarkably consistent. One of these (Cree and Davis, 2007) examined social work in a number of settings. The other (Beresford et al., 2007) looked particularly at social work in palliative care – an area of practice involving work with people who are dying or those who have been bereaved.

RESEARCH SUMMARY

What service users want from social workers

In a three year, national project supported by the Joseph Rowntree Foundation, Beresford and colleagues (2007) asked 111 people who were either dying or had been bereaved what they valued most in palliative care social workers. Three factors emerged:

- *The quality of the relationship between service user and social worker, which should include:*

  - *a genuine relationship;*

  - *friendship and reciprocity;*

RESEARCH SUMMARY *continued*

> – *flexible professional boundaries.*
>
> • *The personal qualities of the social worker.*
>
> • *The nature and process of the work, which included:*
>
> – *time, accessibility, continuity;*
>
> – *being reliable and delivering;*
>
> – *tailoring work to the individual.*
>
> *In a study of mainstream social work practice but where a much smaller number of service users were included (Cree and Davis, 2007), the importance of relationship, reciprocity, listening and the worker's use of self were also strong themes in all service areas.*

It will be useful to bear this evidence in mind as we consider, in Chapter 5, how we respond to service users experiencing loss. Clearly, service users are looking for someone who is prepared to give of their time, to listen and to develop relationships involving some degree of reciprocity. Later in this chapter, we look at some of the issues that this raises for social workers in terms of the impact of their own experience of loss.

Warren (2007) argues that the clear message from reports of service users' views about what they want from social workers is that social workers' personal attributes can make all the difference. The social work role is one that is characterised by a response at both the practical and the emotional level (Cree and Davis, 2007; Currer, 2001). To be effective, social workers must have skills both in building and sustaining relationships and also in responding to particular needs. Since loss is a key aspect of service users' experience in all settings, social workers need the underpinning theory and appropriate interpersonal skills to recognise loss and to respond in an appropriate way.

The need for training to focus on loss and its effects

A number of authors point to the neglect of this topic within training for social work. Thompson (2002a) speaks of its relative neglect and 'invisibility' in the theory base of social work, whilst from Australia, Goldsworthy (2005) suggests that the broad topic of grief and loss has received only 'sporadic attention' in the social work literature, despite its centrality for the profession. Hooyman and Kramer (2006) make the same point from a North American perspective. Part of the reason for this is that the topic of grief and loss has been associated in a narrow way with dying and bereavement, and thus as an issue only for those in specialist areas of practice. Even within the area of social work with people who are dying and bereaved, there has been a tendency, at least in the UK, to ignore dying and bereavement as issues for mainstream practitioners working in community settings (Currer, 2001). Thus a double sidelining has occurred, with the result that loss as a broad issue underpinning the work of all social workers has received little dedicated attention. There is a broad theory base in relation to loss and grief, but this has not found its way into the social work curriculum in a systematic and focused fashion.

Understanding what we are talking about

Defining our terms

If we are to progress further and explore this topic with any precision, we must now pay attention to defining key terms. Definitions provide a starting point for discussion, and they also reveal some discrepancies and questions, as we shall see.

Change

When I looked on the internet for definitions of this frequently used term, I found some common themes, some contradictions and also some commonly occuring links. All are instructive. Change involves difference, movement and alteration from a previous state to a subsequent one. There are differences, however, in how complete this alteration may be. Some define the alteration as one affecting the core characteristics of the situation: terms like 'conversion' or 'transformation' are used. In contrast, sometimes it is emphasised that change does *not* involve becoming 'different in essence' – otherwise this is not a change but something completely different. These are issues that will become important when we consider loss. In some instances, a complete change will be involved; in others this is not so, and this therefore affects a person's response.

I mentioned that there are frequent links associated with the word 'change'. Many of these are to business sites. What is called 'change management' has become an important branch of management science. In the world of business and commerce, people have recognised that change – often continuous and rapid – is as much a key factor in corporate life as in individual lives. You will find that the theories of some influential writers on loss and grief are used as part of this discourse. One that is adopted particularly is the very influential work of Elizabeth Kübler-Ross (1970), whose work on dying will be looked at in Chapter 3. Moreover, management science frequently draws attention to the fact that change – although challenging – can be seen either as loss or as opportunity. Individuals and companies can focus on what things were like before, or on the future and its possibilities. We have already seen in one of the earlier case studies that this can be the case. We will need to bear this in mind when looking in Chapter 3 at models of grieving. Yet the use of theoretical models in different discipline contexts (in this instance in management science and in social work) should not mask the fact that when theories and models of loss and change are applied in different contexts, they may well be accompanied by different ideologies. In the world of business, for example, there is pressure to move forward (to see change as opportunity rather than as loss) – often to enhance productivity or profit. In the areas of counselling and therapy, our overriding concern should be for the wellbeing of the person concerned. There are often different views of what a 'successful outcome' would be. As already mentioned, issues of definition can draw our attention to key issues and themes. In the case of change, we need to identify both the overall cultural pressures and also individual personality differences in the way that change is perceived and approached. This is perhaps a good place to stop for a moment and consider how you usually see change – as opportunity, or threat?

ACTIVITY 1.2

Think of a recent incident when you were expected to change your plans or work arrangements. This might be at work or at home. Spend a few moments thinking about your own reactions and responses.

> *Do you initially resist change? In what ways? Why is this?*

> *Does your response alter as you get more used to the idea?*

> *Do you fall in with change, but feel resentful?*

Make a note of your responses.

Comment

Sociologist Peter Marris (1986) suggests that we resist change because of something he has called the *conservative impulse*. This is defined as *the impulse to defend the predictability of life*, which he suggests is *a fundamental and universal principle of human psychology* (Marris, 1986, p2). This links to ideas of *ontological security* developed by Giddens (1991). *Ontological security* is the sense of being safe and secure in the world – in popular terms we might describe it as 'knowing where we are and what's what'. Resistance to change is therefore a normal reaction, although there are individual differences in the extent to which change threatens us. One much used personality inventory is based on research that shows that some people are more interested in possibilities than certainties, and hence more open to change. You have perhaps also noted that it makes a difference who suggests the change and whether you have been involved in bringing it about. Change may also be less resisted if the need for it is explained – in other words, if we can see the meaning that it has. Can you see how the themes of coherence and control (mentioned above in the first section of this chapter) are coming into play here?

Loss

Change is a neutral term – it can be positive or negative – whilst loss is the term used to refer to disadvantageous or detrimental aspects of a change. As Hooyman and Kramer state: *Losses ... always result in deprivation of some kind; in essence, we no longer have someone or something that we used to have* (2006, p2). If change is about alteration and adjustment, loss is also about absence. Loss is frequently associated with death – a study reported by Harvey (1998) found that 60% of American college students associated this word with a death – but is actually a much more general term, and it is in this general sense that it is used throughout this book. As we shall see later in this chapter, we can start to identify different aspects of loss as a way to also identify some key characteristics within the broad concept. Although the experience of loss is very individual, such key dimensions will be helpful as a starting point in our attempt to understand what loss may mean in a particular situation.

Grief

Like 'loss', the term 'grief' is now frequently associated with death. However, its origins are much broader, and this narrow interpretation is relatively recent. Goss and Klass (2005) recount how in definitions from 1913, the term not only included pain resulting from a broad range of losses, but also referred to the cause of the suffering itself. There are similarities with the current colloquial use of the term 'don't give me grief'. Between then and now a dual movement took place, narrowing the term to a connection with the pain following a death, and also seeing grief as an individual psychological process. Such changing understandings alert us to facets of the social context within which all scholarship and communication are inevitably located. In this book, a broad usage will be adopted in terms of the nature of the loss giving rise to grief. Yet I will also be careful not to assume that research findings relating to one type of loss experience apply across the whole range. In the recent eagerness to rediscover loss as a broad range of experiences, there can be a tendency to state without question that research findings relating to death are applicable to a broad range of losses. We must exert caution here. As we shall see when we look at ways in which losses can be categorised, death is not only, as some authors assert, the ultimate loss. It is also a very distinctive loss. In taking a broad approach to loss and grief, I shall therefore take care to specify the research base, and will leave open the question of whether findings can be applied across areas of loss, except where I am aware that this has been tested.

What, then, is 'grief'? Again, differences in definitions are as instructive as the definitions themselves. Fahlberg (1991, p141, cited in Howe, 1995, p58) suggests that *grief is the process through which one passes in order to recover from a loss*. Other authors would questions whether it is right to speak of 'recovery' in this context. Thus, Marris speaks of grieving as the *psychological process of adjustment to loss* (1986, p4). In other words, grief is not something that we just 'get over' like flu. Significant losses become a part of our life, and increasingly, authors (see, for example, the relevant chapters in Neimeyer, 2001) are focusing upon growth as an outcome of grieving, and not just a return to a previous status quo. This issue – apparent from attempts to define the term – is one to which we will return in Chapter 3.

Another key issue in understanding 'grief' is whether it is in the heart or the mind – a primarily emotional or a primarily cognitive process. Thus we have the following definition from 1998:

> *Grief is the primarily emotional reaction to the loss of a loved one through death, which incorporates diverse psychological and physical symptoms and is sometimes associated with detrimental health consequences.* (Stroebe and Schut, 1998, p7)

Note the focus here upon the loss of a person, through death, and on emotional reaction and psychological and physical 'symptoms'. Others concentrate upon the construction and reconstruction of meaning (a cognitive process), and on social aspects. Thus, Klass, Silverman and Nickman see grief as about *construction and reconstruction of a world and of our relationships with others* (1996, p20). Neimeyer argues that *meaning is as much a social practice as it is a cognitive process* (2001, p6). Such is the rate of theory development in this field that Stroebe and Schut (the authors of the quotation above) have recently looked at the cognitive aspects of their own model (2001).

ACTIVITY 1.3

Take a moment to consider your own response to a recent loss. Can you identify aspects of mental activity – seeking for meaning – as well as emotional and physical reactions? Which was predominant in your experience? Do you think it is better to speak of 'adjustment' or 'recovery', and can you identify aspects of personal growth in your grief, as well as pain?

Comment

This activity was designed to make the different arguments in this section real for you. There are no 'right' answers, and you may like to explore the issues further by comparing your responses with those of a colleague. Already, we are beginning to explore aspects of theory.

Mourning

'Mourning' is a term that is very close to 'grief', and they are used interchangeably by some authors. The focus of mourning is usually upon the social aspects of grieving, such as collective rituals, which will be considered in more detail in the next chapter. Mourning is usually associated with death-related losses, and with customary social responses. As grief becomes more broadly defined to incorporate social as well as psychological aspects, there is an increasing overlap in terminology.

Bereavement

'Bereavement' is a term used for loss through death. The word has its roots in a word meaning to 'rob', suggesting that bereavement is when a person is taken from us.

Bearing in mind changes in the ways in which 'grief' is being used and understood, as outlined above, the difference between these three terms has been usefully summarised as follows: *Bereavement is an event, grief is the emotional process, mourning is the cultural process* (Oliviere et al., 1998, p121).

Service users/experts though experience

Before leaving the definition of terms, I would like to add a word here about my use of the term 'service users'. I started this chapter by asserting the importance of the fact that we all have experience of loss. Whilst this is true, we do not all use social work or other services at times of loss. For this reason, I distinguish in this context between what I will call 'experts by experience' (following Cairney at al., 2006) and 'service users'. Since we all experience loss, the latter term incorporates the former, but not vice versa. It is perhaps worth noting that this issue arose for me in a practical way in relation to my teaching – I have for many years encouraged students on the 'Loss and Social Work' course to draw upon their own knowledge and expertise in relation to issues of loss, and this has formed a rich basis for learning and discussion. However, it has also been valuable to invite service users into the classroom to tell us of their experiences concerning the ways in which professional workers have responded to their loss issues in a service context. Whilst some students had their own experiences as service users, not all did. Becoming a user of services is a distinct experience that may itself bring attendant additional losses as well as potential gains.

Ways of categorising loss

I suggested earlier that we would look at some key dimensions that help us to 'categorise' losses. One of the earliest distinctions was between physical and symbolic loss (see Rando, 1988). Whilst physical loss refers to something or someone tangible that is no longer present, symbolic losses are abstract changes in the way that life is experienced, such as a loss of status or self-image. We have already considered some symbolic losses when we looked at the situation of redundancy. I wonder if you can think of other ways in which losses may vary.

ACTIVITY 1.4

Dimensions of loss

Think about three or four specific situations of loss and see if you can identify ways in which they differ from each other, and ways in which they are similar.

Comment

Different authors have drawn attention to a number of aspects of loss which affect the way it is experienced. In thinking about these dimensions of loss it is important that we do not fall into the trap of assuming that one type of loss is inevitably 'worse' or 'more difficult' than another. For the moment, just concentrate on thinking about these as ways of describing different situations of loss, and perhaps about how the categories may overlap.

When the loss is not final

One of the differences that may have occurred to you is the difference between a loss that is final and one that is not. For example, losing a partner, child or parent through death is a different situation to losing a partner through divorce or separation. Leaving aside any beliefs about a possible reunion after death, one situation involves the possibility of ongoing actual contact (and perhaps many goodbyes or partings), while the other does not. A number of different and overlapping terms have been used to draw attention to this difference.

Bruce and Schultz refer to *nonfinite loss* to describe *losses that are contingent on development; the passage of time; and on a lack of synchrony with hopes, wishes, ideals and expectations* (2001, p7). These losses are ones with no clear end – the authors here use the term to refer to the grief that may be associated with long-term disability or situations as disparate as sexual abuse, infertility, divorce and adoption.

Boss (1999; 2006) uses the term *ambiguous loss* to describe those losses which do not have finality and therefore cannot be resolved. Within *ambiguous loss*, Boss distinguishes situations of physical presence and psychological absence (such as dementia) from situations where there is physical absence and psychological presence (such as an absent parent following divorce, or a child who has been adopted). Her work is explored in more detail in Chapter 4. In terms of bereavement, Boss's focus is on deaths where there may be no body for burial, in situations such as the Tsunami or the terrorist attacks of 9/11. Yet we might extend her argument to all bereavements, in which the person is physically absent but remains psychologically present. I will suggest in Chapter 3 that this distinction may be more broadly relevant.

The terms non-finite loss and ambiguous loss draw attention to the finality of the experience. We have already noted absence as a feature of loss, but these authors show that such absence may be actual or psychological, permanent or transitory, and may be an absence when compared either with expectation or with a previous presence.

When the loss is uncommon

Child deaths were once a frequent occurrence, now they are rare – at least in the UK. Although we cannot compare the pain experienced in any abstract terms, we do need to note that there is likely to be a different level of understanding from others, and a different level of social support now as compared with the past. This is well illustrated by the setting up of specific self-help groups by those who have had a experienced the death of a child or of a baby, for example. This is frequently done because those concerned wish to be in touch with others who have had a similar experience. When the experience is one that is uncommon, such mutual support may no longer be naturally available within a community.

When the loss is not acknowledged

Some losses cannot be freely spoken of. Doka (1989; 2002) has coined the term *disenfranchised grief* to refer to grief where the griever is seen as not entitled to grieve. This may be for one of three reasons.

- The loss itself may not be regarded by others as serious (the death of a pet might come into this category).

- The relationship may not be one that is recognised socially – a gay partnership or an extra-marital relationship may be the basis for grief that is disenfranchised in this way. Funerals provide a dramatic illustration of this when the person who was closest to the deceased may hear of the death by a roundabout route (if at all) and will be excluded from plans or from the rituals. This also occurs when such a relationship ends in other ways – a person may not be able to tell others of their loss if the relationship was a hidden one.

- Finally, the person themselves may be a member of a category of persons who are commonly seen as less likely to grieve or to grieve deeply. This might apply to children who are often seen to 'get over it quickly', to those with a learning disability who it may be said 'do not understand' or to older people who are 'used to it'.

'It's your own fault' – the issue of choice

Losses may be socially unacceptable for other reasons. Generally speaking, there is less public sympathy for any loss that is seen to have been something that the person concerned has 'brought on themselves'. For example, the events of spontaneous miscarriage and termination of pregnancy have an identical outcome, but one was 'chosen' whilst the other was not. I have placed the word 'chosen' in inverted commas to indicate that this may well be a choice made under pressure, but nevertheless, it is seen to be different from an event that 'just happens'. This aspect of loss is very important in determining the responses that people have – including the response of the person concerned. There may be comfort in thinking that 'there was nothing I could have done' and sometimes guilt in thinking 'it was my decision'. In the media we can see that any hint of responsibility can lead to a lack of understanding, and to blame. Even in cases of terminal illnesses or of war we read of 'innocent victims' – for example, those who contract AIDs through blood transfusions or those who are caught up in conflict through 'no fault of their own'. The implication is that a soldier who dies in conflict has 'signed up', and a person engaging in a homosexual relationship can expect to become ill as a result. This also applies when we bring pain on ourselves as the result of a choice that we have made.

Many losses that we encounter as social workers have this element. The pain of a parent whose child is removed due to neglect; the loss of freedom that may follow when somebody commits an offence – all these losses may be seen as unworthy of sympathy or even acknowledgement because of the responsibility that the person involved is seen to have for their situation.

ACTIVITY **1.5**

Responsibility for loss

Choose an area of social work practice and list some of the losses that a service user may experience that can be viewed by other people as 'their own fault'. What effects does this perception have on:

- *the way the person sees themselves?*

- *the way they are treated by others?*

- *the way they are treated within the system?*

Comment

As social workers, we need to recognise the power of public perceptions even in some of our own attitudes towards the situations of loss in which service users find themselves. It is important to understand and acknowledge that the pain of loss may be increased (rather than lessened) by such issues of apparent 'choice' and responsibility, because these also impact on the judgements that the person concerned is making about themself.

Finally, we also have to recognise that as social workers we will sometimes be in the position of imposing loss. Although we are aware that decisions about the removal of someone's child or liberty are not ones for which we are in fact individually responsible, this does not lessen the guilt that we may feel, or the fact that others may see us as responsible. Collectively, social workers are periodically portrayed in the media as being responsible for pain and loss that could have been avoided. As we shall see, such aspects of the social work role can lead – at an individual level – to a tendency to deny or avoid the pain that service users experience in order to protect ourselves. It is my hope that this book will help you to identify when this might be happening and to look for other more appropriate ways of responding, whilst also putting in place support systems to help you to manage the pain that you experience yourself through being involved with people who are dealing with trauma and loss.

Recognising our own losses

We come now to consider our own personal losses in more detail and the impact that these may have on our practice. We will look at ways in which our own experiences can be used to enhance our work as professionals. I started this book (see my overall introduction) with a 'health warning'. Loss is an emotive subject, and even studying it, reading reports of research and considering case examples can trigger emotions and thoughts associated with our own experiences. When I am teaching this subject, I ask students to identify a 'buddy' with whom they can discuss any reactions or personal issues that have been raised by the material from each session. As I said before, a book presents a different challenge, because I cannot judge the effect that reading this book may have on you, or ensure that you have adequate personal support as you think about these issues. You may want to look at how to arrange this for yourself. It can be useful to keep a notebook or journal and make a note of the responses that you have to the activities that are part of this book. As I said in the introduction, this has two purposes – it provides a way to 'offload', but also gives you a chance to look back and reflect on your own learning and responses. In this area, more perhaps than any other, you need to develop some habits that will be useful when you encounter these issues in the practice setting. Because I know that you will encounter them in your practice I make no apology for raising such issues here – better to explore your own experience in the comparative 'safety' of a library or your place of study than when you are in the company of a service user who needs your undivided attention.

Your own experience of loss

Social work is emotionally demanding, and it is not easy to be receptive to the hurt that others are experiencing. This can be particularly difficult if their situation reminds us of our own losses, particularly if this catches us unawares at the end of a tiring day. Sometimes these similarities can make us more, rather than less, involved with a particular service user and their situation. One worker tells of how she always found herself putting in extra effort and staying late on behalf of a particular client whose situation represented aspects of her own past. On other occasions these resonances from our own life make us 'push the situation away' in an emotional sense (and possibly the service user with it). For this reason, self-awareness is an essential ingredient for everyone who works with people who are vulnerable or experiencing loss.

ACTIVITY **1.6**

Time line

Draw a horizontal line on a sheet of paper with your current age at the right-hand end and your date of birth on the left. Make a note of the major events that you have experienced at places on the line that represent your age at the time. How many of these included aspects of loss?

Below the line make a note of the losses that were involved, and above the line note the gains that you experienced as a result of each situation. See if you can apply some of the distinctions from this chapter to these events – was this an ambiguous or disenfranchised loss, for example?

Comment

You will probably find that many events have brought both gain and loss. What opportunities did you have to grieve for the losses brought about by these events? For example, at a time of crisis for all the family, one member's grief may be belittled or overlooked. This can also be the case when a change is seen as 'good' by the family overall, but has negative consequences for some members. For example, a parent's new job may have meant more money and a better house, but a change of school for you as a child and the loss of a best friend. Now look at the clustering and pattern of events. Have there been particularly difficult times in your life, when one change or loss has followed quickly on others?

How our own experience can impact on our practice

What sort of assumptions do you tend to make about other people because of your own experiences? For example, if you had to cope, you may think that other people should not make a fuss. Or you may have the opposite reaction – you may think that you would never impose on anyone else a change such as you had to experience. How might these responses influence your reactions to service users? Look back now at Activity 1.2 (on page 15) in which you were asked about your own response to change. Can you see any links between those responses to change and your own history of loss?

The experience of loss in our own lives has the potential to turn us into good practitioners. Even if you feel that you have relatively little experience of loss, this is something that can be helpful in practice if you are aware of your own starting point. The key for all of us is to develop a good awareness of our own background and emotional 'baggage'. Emotional 'baggage' can consist of many experiences of loss, or (just as easily) of a sort of guilty sense of 'I've been so lucky in my life; I want to help those who are not so fortunate'. Both sorts of baggage can get in the way of good practice, or provide good motivation in our work, depending upon how they are handled.

Using our own experience constructively

Three factors are important for the good handling of 'emotional baggage'.

- Awareness – knowing what our own experience has been and how it affects our responses.

- Support – being helped to look at our responses to service users and their losses in a safe environment, in the knowledge that we will receive help to handle issues at work that are difficult for us, either practically or emotionally.

- Development – which includes opportunities to learn more both about ourselves and about our work, with the aim of improving our practice.

Awareness
The next activity asks you to consider the 'boundaries' between the personal and the professional in more detail.

ACTIVITY **1.7**

Given your own background, and reflecting upon your practice experience, what do you see as your own areas of particular strength and vulnerability? Make a list with two columns, headed 'strengths' and 'vulnerable areas'. The following questions may help you to think about this.

- *What was your motivation for entering social work?*

- *Are there areas of social work that you wish to avoid, or that you are especially drawn to work in? Why is this?*

- *What situations in practice elicit your spontaneous sympathy?*

- *What type of person is it hard for you to work with? Why might this be?*

Comment

You may have found quite an overlap between the two columns, with some factors listed as both strengths and weaknesses. Someone once defined a 'weakness' as an 'over-developed strength', and there is much truth in this. For example, your own experience of separation may give you insight into how devastating this can be, but it may also give you a tendency to see the service user's experience through the 'lens' of how you felt. 'Insight in situations of separation' would therefore be listed under strengths, and 'tendency to identify' under vulnerabilities. Avoid judging yourself – our own experiences, backgrounds and personalities are the tools with which we work; they just need to be used appropriately. One aspect of using them appropriately is to be clear about keeping the personal and the professional separate; it is when the boundaries become blurred that we are in danger of imposing our own experiences or assumptions upon others, rather than checking out how they are feeling.

It is not always easy to use our own experiences in a positive and appropriate way and to avoid blurring the boundaries. For one thing, it can be hard to see when we are getting over-involved, or if we are appearing to be disinterested. We need feedback from others about our own behaviour, and our communication. Feedback is the opposite of gossiping behind someone's back; it should be a regular feature of a work environment, and offered in a non-threatening way, in confidence, and in the context of an open and trusting relationship. This contributes to awareness, and comes through supervision, which is one aspect of support. Support is considered next, starting with thinking about ways in which we can help ourselves and then by looking at supervision in more detail.

Support

Support is not an optional extra for social workers. In most cases, we cannot pick and choose what comes up through our work. For example, you may have decided not to work in a hospice, because death is something you do not find very easy to work with. Yet death crops up in all areas of practice. Or you may have avoided work in child protection whilst your own children are young, yet children and issues of abuse arise in all areas of practice. Mental health issues are not restricted to mental health services. So, try as we may, we need to find ways of supporting and protecting our colleagues and ourselves. These should be ways that make us more, rather than less, receptive to the pain felt by service users. I will consider two types of support: things that we can do for ourselves, as well as support from others – which includes supervision.

Helping ourselves

It will quite often happen that we are expected to deal with an emotional situation involving a relationship dispute just after coming to work following a row with a partner. Or we might be arranging care for an older person recovering from surgery after hearing that a parent has to go into hospital. Being aware of our own 'baggage' may be necessary, but how do we deal with it especially when it is very current?

My guess is that you have developed your own ways of doing this. Not all of these ways are helpful, however, so it is worth taking them out and looking at them. For example, simply trying to 'shut off' our emotions totally can make us seem very hard or 'prickly'. It is more useful to see if you can put your own life and its challenges to one side, in a sort of 'pending' tray! Here are some examples of things that students have said work for them.

- *I always imagine locking my home troubles in the car when I turn the key after parking for work. I visualise leaving them there until I come back to them at the end of the day.* Another person reports doing the same when they shut their front door as they leave for work.

- *When I come to work, I have to have a cup of coffee. Then I wander round the Unit to see how things are, before turning to my own work. This is a way of tuning in, and I feel quite upset if I am interrupted before I can do these things. They are a way of switching off from home and being fully present at work.*

- *In my mind, I have a chest of drawers. Work belongs in one drawer, home in another. I can shut one drawer and open another. This enables me to focus upon what I am meant to be doing at the time, and to put the other matters firmly away.*

In some residential settings, there may be a formal 'hand over' meeting, or a daily staff meeting. Routines, whether personal or institutionalised, can be a very useful way of 'managing' or controlling life. We also need 'refreshment' routines during the day. Social workers are renowned for keeping going without taking a lunch break! This can be dangerous for our emotional as well as our physical health – and can also make us very poor practitioners, since we cannot give our best to service users. Here are some refreshment routines that social workers have described to me.

- *I am a smoker; I find that having a cigarette gives me a break periodically.*

- *I am a religious person, and my prayer times in the day are a source of refreshment. I believe that they help me to be a better worker.*

- *There is a particular tree outside my window. I make a point of looking at it, and breathing deeply at regular intervals during the day.*

- *I used to have a sandwich at my desk or in the car. I don't do that anymore. If possible, I eat outside, and take at least half an hour, preferably alone. I am sure that this has improved my practice.*

All of these are ways in which we can 'help ourselves'. Just as important are the support mechanisms that involve other people. Supervision should be a routine feature of social work settings.

Supervision

Supervision has a long and proud tradition in social work; sadly, there is evidence (Thompson, 1999) that its practice is declining – which is ironic, given that the nursing profession is just discovering its importance (Bishop, 1997).

ACTIVITY **1.8**

What system of supervision operates in your workplace?

How adequate do you find it?

Is it possible to acknowledge and discuss your own emotional needs, as well as the allocation and management of work?

What, if anything, needs to change if you are to address the areas of strength and vulnerability already noted?

Comment

There is quite an extensive literature on the issues of supervision in social work – some sources are Browne and Bourne (1996) and Hawkins and Shohet (2000). Lishman (1998, p98) gives a short summary of the issues. Generally, it is accepted that supervision should deal with both caseload management (the management of work) and with the emotional needs of workers.

In relation to paying attention to your emotional needs, this might involve asking you to reflect upon your responses to particular service users and their situations. We have seen that service users value relationships in which social workers use themselves, are there for them, and 'go the extra mile' (Beresford et al., 2007; Cree and Davis, 2007). It is only possible to use the self in this way if we are supported through effective supervision (Cree and Davis, 2007). The alternative is a worker who always 'plays it by the book' and offers nothing of the human relationship that can be essential in establishing genuine trust. This may be safe, but it is unlikely to be much help. Supervision that pays attention to emotional issues also safeguards the service user from abuse, by alerting us to situations where we might be getting our personal and professional boundaries blurred.

Clearly, this type of supervision needs to be in the context of a relationship in which you feel comfortable (whether or not this is a line manager) and at a regular, dedicated time, if it is to be effective.

If these features are not in place, it is very doubtful that you will be able be work to your full potential with people experiencing loss, and your practice may even be (unconsciously) harmful. If you are in a management position, you may be able to establish such conditions within your team (this may involve an outside consultant or counsellor), or to insist upon such conditions in service contracts for work that is contracted out. Private companies providing care also need to offer appropriate support to standards that enable workers to do their job safely.

Strong words, perhaps? If such support or supervision is not in place, what can you do, apart from lobbying for change? You might give some thought to formalising a system of peer support. This could take the form of agreeing with a colleague that you will review your work together at regular intervals. If you are not receiving adequate formal supervision, it is perfectly legitimate to see such mutual support as a 'work activity' for which time can be set aside in working hours. You will need to agree with each other how the time will be spent and about when and where to meet. Again, this needs to be time set aside, in a place where you can speak freely and privately. The boundaries of confidentiality will also have to be agreed, as in any form of supervision. You can be sure that time set aside for such mutual support will be well spent, and will enhance your practice with service users experiencing loss.

Training and development

As registered social workers, our continued registration and codes of practice include a requirement to engage in ongoing professional development. This is important in relation to loss as in relation to other areas of practice. It is a way of being periodically refreshed, as well as keeping up to date with new theoretical ideas. In the area of loss, for example, there has been a great deal of new research in the past ten years or so, as we shall see in Chapter 3. For many practitioners who qualified some time ago, there is a pressing need to update their understanding in line with this new research and development.

Reflecting on your responses to Activity 1.7 (see page 23), it might be helpful to use your journal to identify your own training or development needs at this point in time. For example, you might need to do some work on anger management, or to look more deeply at some area of loss that is having an effect on your life and work but that was previously 'buried'. There are also courses on managing stress that might enhance your repertoire of self-help techniques.

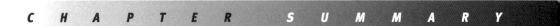

C H A P T E R S U M M A R Y

In this chapter, we have seen that loss and change are part of everyday life for all of us. For those who use social work services, loss is likely to be a key aspect of current or past experience. Therefore all social workers need to be able to identify situations of loss and should be able to use up-to-date theoretical models within their practice. In addition, our own experience of loss can be used creatively as part of good practice, although it can also be harmful if we are not self-aware and well-supported.

The chapter has offered some definitions of terms, which will be further developed and expanded in subsequent chapters. We have noted that loss involves both alteration and absence. This absence may be actual or psychological. It may be temporary or permanent. We have also seen that a loss brings implications or secondary losses, and that these too may be practical or abstract. The significance of loss is an important dimension, and the same situation or loss may have different meaning or significance for those involved.

We then identified the question of control. This may be control over the event itself – whether it could have been prevented – or it may concern the extent of control over implications. Choice is an issue that links with control.

Lastly, we have seen that there are questions to be asked about the desirable outcome following a loss – do we hope to return to how we were before it, or do we perhaps hope for more than this – that the experience of loss, though painful, may lead to growth? Overall, do we focus on the past, or the future?

I hope that this chapter has convinced you of the importance of this topic, whatever your area of current or future practice, as well as raising some of the questions that will be explored in later chapters.

FURTHER READING

Thompson, N (ed) (2002a) Introduction, in Thompson, N (ed) *Loss and grief: a guide for human services practitioners*. Basingstoke: Palgrave.

This book is a very useful and accessible overview that has chapters on loss that relate to a number of areas of social work practice. The introductory chapter is especially relevant for the issues raised here. Others will be referred to in relation to later chapters.

Bright, R (1996) *Grief and powerlessness*. London: Jessica Kingsley.

Written by a music therapist, this book also covers a range of losses and offers a good introduction to the topic overall.

Cree, V and Davis, A (2007) *Social work: voices from the inside*. London: Routledge.

Although this book is not about loss specifically, it offers an excellent way in to social work from the perspectives of social workers and service users, showing how the quality of a relationship is central for both.

Chapter 2
Loss and grief in a social and cultural context

Introduction

The pain of loss is such that it is usually experienced as being intensely lonely and isolating. Even when the loss we suffer is one that affects others too, it is often the case that we feel that our feelings and experiences are unique – that no-one else could possibly understand.

At one level, this is true. Yet loss is in many ways a socially defined experience. Field, Hockey and Small argue that *age, ethnicity, gender, social class and sexuality all profoundly affect the ways people experience death, dying and bereavement* (1997, p1). This appears to be so in relation to other losses too, although there is less systematic research evidence to draw upon here, so we shall not take the parallels for granted.

All societies have expectations of those who grieve, as well as rituals and customs that may offer some comfort in grief and define socially acceptable behaviour for those who are grieving and for those around them. The purpose of this chapter is to ensure that our consideration of models and theories of grieving – which are the subject of Chapter 3 – is grounded in a recognition that experiences of loss and of grief, although intensely personal, are also socially patterned, negotiated and regulated. We have already noted some social variations in the ways in which loss may be experienced in Chapter 1; here we will turn to the disciplines of sociology and anthropology to look at these issues in greater depth, and to identify the perspectives and concepts that these disciplines can offer to the social worker who is interested in understanding more about loss and grief.

There are six main sections to this chapter. Most draw upon comparisons – over time or between societies – to highlight the existence of social and cultural variations, and also to help us to identify underlying patterns and issues. The first looks in detail at the need for a broad view as a basis for practice with individuals. The next section looks at how statistical patterns of loss (in this instance of suicide) may be related to overall social factors, and at the argument that the nature of a society – and of a person's place within it – affects an individual's experience of loss. The third section considers ways in which losses are socially defined and classified. Even in the case of death, some deaths are seen as 'good deaths' whilst others are seen as 'bad deaths'. In relation to other losses, it may even be that what is seen in one society as a loss is not seen as such in another. Next, we will consider the ways in which responses to loss are socially determined, looking at the nature and function of customs and rituals. We will then look at how grief and loss are socially regulated at individual and political levels. Lastly, we will consider the implications of this for social work practice.

You may yourself have personal experience of more than one culture or society, or memories of times when grief was differently handled. If so, this will mean that you are already aware of some of the issues of diversity that will be highlighted in this chapter. I hope that this will be a resource that enhances your learning, and that concepts and perspectives from sociology and anthropology will give you ways of speaking about some of these differences and applying this personal knowledge to your practice with people experiencing loss.

Thinking broadly about loss

It is important that our practice is informed by a broadly-based view of loss, because this links with the social work commitment to practice that is truly anti-oppressive. If it is to be more than mere 'political correctness', such a commitment must be underpinned by an understanding of the social forces that mould experience and behaviour for all of us – not just those from minority groups. It is not always easy to take a broad view of this particular topic, because it has, in the past, been dominated by an individual focus.

Dominance of an individual focus

Studies of grief have tended to focus on death and dying. Within this body of literature, social and cultural issues have tended, until recently, to be ignored by those who have studied grief and loss (Field et al., 1997; Howarth, 2007). It is worth stopping for a moment to consider the reason for this. Some have suggested that the study of death has been sidelined within sociology (Wilmott, 2000), but in fact some of the earliest sociological writers did look at death and dying. For example, Emile Durkheim published a classic study of suicide in 1897, whilst Glaser and Strauss later reported on studies of dying in texts published in the 1960s – we will use their insights in a later chapter. Others have taken a broad historical or sociological perspective (such as Gorer, 1965 and Ariès 1974; 1981) or have looked on the individual experience of loss and grief from a sociological starting point (Marris, 1986). Yet the literature for practitioners has concentrated on the internal world and the feelings of grieving individuals. And because the research base has tended to be about grief in European or American contexts and populations, issues of difference or variation in the experience of loss within other cultures have tended to be ignored until recently.

The dominance of an individualist focus in academic work on grief – especially in relation to dying – cannot entirely be explained by a lack of sociological interest in the subject, although this may be part of the story. Another part of the explanation is itself cultural, and relates to the overall climate of individualism in the Western world. As we shall see, interest in the subject of death takes different forms in different societies and at different times (Walter, 1994). Interest in individual grief and pain is a sign of our times, and has permeated what we study and how. In other times or places, people would have been far more interested in the welfare of the dead than in the pain of the living, or in the passing on of leadership roles within a community rather than the memory of a single person (Goss and Klass, 2005). As we enter the 'postmodern' era, there is now more interest in diversity, and although there is still a focus on the individual, this takes a different form (Giddens, 1991). We shall see how this theoretical orientation has affected the 'received wisdom' in relation to grief and loss.

The focus in practice-related work on grief in the second half of the twentieth century has then been on individual experience, and cross cultural and critical perspectives have not been so apparent. Recent texts and scholarship (e.g. Holloway, 2007a) have begun to redress this balance so that models of grief and loss for practitioners – at least, for those working with people who are dying and bereaved – now draw upon a broader knowledge base, as we shall see in the next chapter.

Why we need a broader view to underpin practice

A focus upon individual experience has implications for social work practice. As you will be aware, cultural and structural factors are key elements in anti-discriminatory practice (Thompson, 2001). Values of anti-oppressive and anti-racist practice are central to social work. Both are rooted in the importance of respect for persons, and recognise that our social and cultural heritage and context are part of who we are. Basing our work on psychology alone can lead to a lack of awareness of the broader social forces that determine or influence individual feeling and behaviour. In addition to their importance in giving us a good knowledge base in relation to recognising our own assumptions and prejudices, the disciplines of sociology and anthropology also draw attention to a number of concepts that will help us to understand individual responses – we will look in what follows at social cohesion or integration, at the functions of customs and rituals and at the idea of 'social death'. It is clear that even what is considered to be loss cannot be taken for granted, and we will look at the ways in which loss is socially managed as well as at issues of power and control.

What sociology and anthropology contribute

At the start of this book, I emphasised that loss is something that we all experience, and that this gives rise to one of the overall problems that we can encounter when we study any kind of human behaviour – particularly when we do so in order to inform our work as practitioners. We are part of the society that we study, and we have our own ideas about it already, as well as our own experiences. Cree (2000) argues that sociology gives us ways to look at what lies behind our taken-for-granted assumptions about social life by helping us to see behaviours in an historical and cultural context. As practitioners, it is easy to become very involved with the people we work with and their situations, and also their ways of understanding them. Sociology and anthropology give us some critical distance on taken-for-granted ways of seeing the world by showing that people in different historical and cultural contexts see things quite differently. What is more, different societies manage common problems and issues in different ways. Basic social institutions (such as the family) take many different forms across the world and over time. Not only is our attention drawn to such diversity, sociologists also ask what it is that maintains different structures – whose interests are served by the different ways in which society is arranged, and how does change come about?

Shared understandings of what is expected and right form the backdrop against which families and individuals identify, express and manage their own losses – where they turn for help and what they expect of others. They also shape social policy because they influence the collective response. Thus they determine the public provision within which social workers may be employed. Shared understandings are often expressed through customs and rituals – these offer a window onto issues of grief and loss, and also point to 'postmodern' society as one in which these matters are often uncertain or disputed. At times of grief and pain, it is important to say or do 'the right thing', but this may be ill-defined in a society in which there has ceased to be a single, recognised authority.

Social determinants of loss

We take our starting point from one of the most famous early sociologists, Emile Durkheim (1858–1917), who was interested in looking at the relationship between the individual and society. He chose to compare the patterns of suicide in different countries and to seek an explanation of differences, not in factors of motivation – an individual, psychological explanation – but in broader social 'facts', such as the person's place in society and the nature of social relationships. I have chosen to start here because I hope it will detach us from that individualistic focus which I have already said has been dominant in thinking about loss and grief. From thinking about how the nature of society affects human behaviour, we will then draw upon the work of a more recent sociologist, Peter Marris, who has considered the ways in which a person's place in society may determine the extent of the loss that they experience.

Suicide: from Durkheim to the present

Suicide is an act that is found in all societies, and which epitomises loss – it brings about loss of life for the person concerned, and complicated and intense grief for those who survive. It may be seen as arising from a sense of loss. On the one hand, suicide is the most individual – even anti-social – of acts. Yet it is also strongly socially regulated, both ideologically (through religion, for example) and legally. Assisting someone to take their own life (often known as PAS or 'physician assisted suicide') is legal in certain European countries and has recently been hotly debated in Britain. As well as being socially regulated, Durkheim argued that suicide rates were linked to social factors, as we can see below.

RESEARCH SUMMARY

Emile Durkheim looked at different rates of suicide in different countries. He found that:

- *Suicide rates were higher for those widowed, single and divorced than married.*

- *Suicide rates were higher for people without children than with children.*

- *Suicide rates were higher amongst Protestants than Catholics.*

He proposed that differences were related both to the method of recording a death by the coroner, and to the factors of 'social integration' and 'social regulation'. He suggested that Protestant societies had lower levels of social integration and regulation than Catholic ones, thus accounting for the differences in rates.

In addition, Durkheim distinguished four types of suicide, which he called:

- *egoistic suicide – when ties between the individual and society are weak (he suggested that divorced men might fall in this category);*

- *altruistic suicide – where ties between the individual and society are so strong that a person may die for others (either because they feel a burden, or to further a cause);*

- *'anomic' suicide – where rapid social change has led to weak social regulation; individuals do not feel that the norms or laws of society have any relationship to their own life goals;*

- *fatalistic suicide – where social regulation is so strong that people feel this is their only escape from oppressive structures or relationships.*

(Durkheim 1951 [1897])

Following Durkheim's work, it came to be taken for granted that suicide could be expected more amongst those who are socially marginalised, an assumption which Prior (1989) questioned on the basis of his own study of death in Belfast. Nevertheless, Durkheim's work drew attention to the links between the individual and society, in contrast to the usual focus of attention, which tended to be, then as now, on aspects of individual motivation. The next activity brings the subject into more recent focus and asks you to do the same.

ACTIVITY **2.1**

Consider the following quotation:

... many countries show a considerable to very strong increase in the frequency of suicide in the 15–29 year age group over the past two decades. This tendency is stronger for males than for females. (Crepet et al., 1992)

Make some suggestions as to the possible reasons for this increase in suicide amongst young men. You may wish to relate your suggestions to Durkheim's research.

Comment

Suicide is an individual act. Clearly statistics are made up of individual tragedies, such as a broken relationship or lost job that may be the 'last straw' for a particular individual. Over a whole population, however, the trends or overall changes in level force us to ask questions, not about individuals but about groups. Some have suggested that the rise in rates of suicide amongst young men may reflect a situation where models of masculinity (what it means to be a man) have become uncertain. This may be combined with unemployment, and lead to a social climate in which many cannot find meaning. This is more than a crisis affecting one particular youngster, and any interpretation should not be sought only within his particular social circle, with the accompanying individual blame or guilt, but also has a broader social context. You might think that there are possible parallels with Durkheim's category of 'anomic suicide'. Concepts of social integration or 'cohesion', questions of identity and economic pressures, may all be seen as relevant.

The social structuring of uncertainty: issues of power

Another sociologist, Peter Marris (1991), suggests that societies differ in the degree of inequality that exists and also in the extent to which attachments are protected and nurtured, and that these factors have an impact on the amount of loss to which individuals in any society are subject. This links to Durkheim's argument that the degree of social integration in a society may be a protective factor in relation to the experience of despair (and hence of loss). Marris also looked at the ways in which inequalities in society may lead to some people experiencing more loss than others. In Chapter 1, the contrast between the experiences of Mary and Joan (see page 7) gave us one example of this. Here is another.

> ## CASE STUDY
>
> *You work in a support service for people with mental health problems. One of your service users has recently found a job in a supermarket. She is late for work on three days running and loses the job as a consequence.*
>
> *She is vulnerable to this situation for a number of reasons. Firstly, she has no car, and is reliant on buses. Secondly, she lives in a rural area and the local bus service only runs once an hour. She has to catch the 6.35 a.m. bus to be at work for 8 a.m. even though the journey only takes 40 minutes. Thirdly, because of her history of mental health problems, her employers attribute her absence to her history of mental illness. Even when she explains that she missed the bus, this is not seen as bad luck but as a lack of planning.*
>
> *An employee with a car could be at work in a much shorter time. A normal 'slippage' of five minutes could be easily accommodated without disastrous consequences. Someone living in an area with better public services would have a more frequent bus service, and if she had no history of mental illness, her explanations might have received a more sympathetic hearing.*

Marris (1991) argues that in society, uncertainty is socially structured. Uncertainty and disruption give rise to loss. Not everyone experiences the same amount of uncertainty and disruption in their lives. He gives examples of the ways in which those with less power and control may have to disrupt their own plans to accommodate those with more power and control – for example, an employer may ask their assistant to stay on at the end of the day to work on some papers when that person had little to do earlier in the day. At a societal level, certain groups of employees (such as those doctors who qualify overseas) are admitted to the medical profession in greater or smaller numbers depending on the availability of recruits – in the past particularly male recruits – from the UK.

You can probably see the relevance of Marris's argument to social work practice. As social workers, we are often working with people who have little power and few financial resources. Not only does this mean that they are vulnerable to secondary losses following a major loss (as in the case of Joan, in Chapter 1), it also means that they are likely to experience more uncertainty in their lives, and therefore more frequent loss overall. You should note that points about the characteristics of a society in overall terms are different from arguments about the amount of social support that any individual may have. It is possible to be well supported within a society that is not supportive overall, and vice versa.

However personal the experience of loss, it is to some extent the product of social circumstances – even in the case of something like suicide. As practitioners, we need to be constantly aware of the ways in which the lives of those we work with are determined or affected by social circumstances that are beyond their control.

Defining the nature of loss

In Chapter 1, we defined loss as the absence of *someone or something that we used to have*. We should note that loss may also be the absence of something that we expected or wanted to have – of dreams and aspirations for a 'perfect child' (if a child is born with a disability, for example) or even a loving parent (in a situation of abuse or an absent parent). You may remember that I referred to 'symbolic losses' as well as to 'ambiguous loss'. Loss is therefore linked to shared understandings of what is expected or desirable.

We have already noted as well that both the rarity of a situation and its acceptability have an effect upon the experience of loss. When a loss is a frequent occurrence, there are expected ways of dealing with it, and there may be good social support. Where it is rarer or taboo, this may not be so. However, situations also become re-defined as society changes. For example, increasing numbers of children are now born outside marriage in the UK – the proportion having increased from 12% in 1980 to 42% in 2004, according to the Office for National Statistics (**www.news.bbc.co.uk**, 21 February 2006). In Victorian society, a baby born outside marriage was a matter for shame and concealment. For a woman in the lower classes it could mean the loss of her home and livelihood; for one in the upper classes, of her reputation and future prospects of marriage. Similarly, changes in the way that homosexuality is perceived are slowly altering the climate within which parents will respond when a child comes out as 'gay'. These situations remain complex, but they demonstrate the way in which changes in social perceptions alter the definition of expectations and of 'normality' and hence what is to be considered to be loss.

Such changing definitions of loss are perhaps more apparent in situations that are not death related, since death is regarded as a loss in most societies, but even here we will see there is considerable variation in the ways in which deaths may be socially defined. We turn next to look at 'good deaths' and 'bad deaths' before looking at other areas of loss.

Defining and categorising death

Sociologist Tony Walter (1994) has given us three 'ideal types' of death characteristic of different societies which he describes as the *traditional*, the *modern* and the *neo-modern*. These time periods refer to Western societies (although some parallels may be observed elsewhere in the world), and may be seen as roughly corresponding to the time prior to the Enlightenment (before about 1600), between that period and the 1950s, and lastly what other authors have called 'postmodern or late modern' society, from the early twentieth century until the present. These epochs overlap and their dates are disputed, but Walter's argument does not rest on precision in this respect. His argument is that these periods were associated with different types of death which were partly the result of the ways in which people died, and were associated with the presence or lack of medical knowledge but which were also linked to shared assumptions about the right way to die, about who should be present and in charge of events, about what happened at the time of death and how mourners should behave. In traditional societies, the authority was religious, represented by a male priest. In modern society, medicine, in the person of a male doctor, was the authority, whilst in contemporary Western societies, there is a new focus upon the self, on personalised and individualised death, with a counsellor (probably female) as the one who is seen as the expert.

Other authors have also noted the demise of the church as the authority on matters of life and death and the medicalisation of death. Barley refers to a wide range of societies in which there may be an emphasis in death on either *dying well, killing splendidly or mourning modestly* (1995, p9), noting that modern Western societies have focused on the latter. Dying well, in the medieval period, was an art form, with religious books and pamphlets on the subject (Howarth, 2007). We can also see the 'good death' in other societies and cultures: here is a description from the Lugbara people in Uganda.

CASE STUDY

A man should die in his hut, lying on his bed, with his brothers and sons around him to hear his last words; he should die with his mind still alert and should be able to speak if only softly; he should die peacefully and with dignity, without bodily discomfort or disturbance ... he should die loved and respected by his family.

(Middleton, 1982, cited in Bradbury, 1993, p68)

The next activity asks you to think about your own ideas about the 'good death'. Try to think first not about what you would like for yourself, but also about what society views as a 'good death'.

ACTIVITY 2.2

Think about ideas of 'the good death' in a society with which you are familiar, and ask what would be a 'bad death'. Can you see any themes? If you have knowledge of more than one society, repeat this for both or all.

Then think about your own wishes and aspirations – are they the same as the cultural ideas you have identified?

'Good deaths', 'bad deaths' 'natural and unnatural deaths'

Walter suggests (1994, p48) that in traditional society, a good death was one where the dying person was conscious and 'ready to meet their maker'. Authority was vested in the Church, and the local priest. In the 'modern period', medicine provided the framework of authority and expertise, and a 'good death' was sudden or when someone was unconscious. A person aspired to be 'no bother to others'. Now, he suggests, the emphasis has changed again – the aim is to do it 'my way', to finish our business with others, maybe with the help of counsellors. The good death is again conscious and aware – as for the Lugbara – but in a very different way.

Mary Bradbury (1993; 1999) has looked in more detail at contemporary ideas of the 'good' and 'bad' death. She argues that these categories are the outcome of a process of negotiation and distinguishes (1993):

- the sacred 'good death' – which is somewhat different to the traditional version;

- 'medicalised' good death;

- the 'natural good death'.

'Good deaths' are usually those where some control can be exercised – this is no less true in other societies than in contemporary Britain, but the nature of control takes a different form in a medicalised culture. In contrast, 'bad deaths' are those that happen in the wrong place at the wrong time. Untimely deaths – an example in contemporary modern society would be that of a child (although in times and places with a high infant mortality, these were more expected and 'normal') – are also usually seen as 'bad deaths'. The category of 'natural deaths' identified by Bradbury from bereaved relatives' accounts is interesting because these deaths were sometimes sudden or unexpected but were desirable because of the absence of fear or pain. This may have been something that you identified in the last activity. She sees this identification of a natural death as 'good' as a modern secular development (it contrasts with earlier ideas that such unexpected deaths were 'bad'). The modern version reinterprets being in control as accepting nature.

Bradbury also alerts us to the importance of asking 'good for whom?' You will no doubt be familiar with situations where a sudden death has been seen by those concerned as good for the person who died but very distressing for those who remain. To this mix we need to add that the perspectives of professionals and of the bereaved may differ, and that, for caregivers (formal or informal), the idea of whether a death was a 'good one' will incorporate their views of the care given – whether they did all they could, for example (Kellehear, 1990).

Clashes of perspective arise in Howarth's (2007) consideration of the management of sudden death. In some societies, the important issue in cases of sudden or unexpected death concerns matters of witchcraft. In modern Britain, it is the coroners office that is charged with the responsibility of investigating sudden deaths, and distinguishing death as being from natural or unnatural causes. The category of 'unnatural death' includes those where there is evidence of human agency, intent or motivation, but it also includes 'accidental death' where there is no human responsibility or control identified. The task of the coroner is to determine 'how, when and where' but not 'why', and because of this there may be tension between relatives and the coroner's office. For those who are bereaved, making some sense of what happened may be paramount, so there can be a gulf between their expectations and the task of the coroner's office (Howarth, 2007, p170). In this and other situations and societies, deaths that are seen as 'senseless' are often perceived to be 'bad deaths'.

An important theme which most authors ignore is that of ontology (the study of meaning) – in this case, what death means to the dying person. Holloway (2007a) explores concepts of death within different religious traditions, but also within broader concepts such as death as darkness, light, transition – ideas that may exist in religions and cut across them. She alerts us to the fact that personal meaning and public religion may not coincide – a point made also by Gunaratnam (1997). Many people without an explicit religious allegiance have strong spiritual beliefs and ideas about death.

Underlying themes and issues
The need to make sense of a death seems to be common to most societies, whether the interpretation is in the form of accusations of witchcraft, or the failure of medical personnel to diagnose early enough or respond appropriately, or within a broader religious or

other framework. Belief systems, which may or may not be expressed in terms of allegiance to a formalised religion, are systems of meaning, and therefore need to be considered in any attempt to understand how loss is viewed. The wish for some form of control also seems to be common, although again the form of control that is seen to be appropriate will vary at different times and in different places. We can see the part played by shared expectations too. I hope that you can identify here those themes of coherence (meaning) and control that were highlighted in the last chapter, as well as gaining a good sense of the variability of understandings and aspirations that may exist – both between societies and within a particular situation also.

Losses other than death

We have seen how ideas of the 'good death' can be an important influence on how people perceive one type of loss, and that shared expectations play a part in this. Death is a particular type of loss, but other losses also relate to matters about which people have shared expectations and aspirations. We can think, for example, of notions of 'the good parent' or 'the good child'. Our understanding of what constitutes a loss depends in part on what we might hope for or expect. These expectations are often so much a part of us that we do not think to question them, until something challenges our taken-for-granted assumptions.

The smiling bride

My eldest daughter was recently married, and in her wedding pictures she is smiling broadly. I also have an old photograph of my great-great-grandmother on her wedding day. Her wedding picture is very different to that of my daughter, because she is not smiling. It was customary for Victorian brides to look very solemn, and this photograph reminds me of the photo of my niece on her wedding day, because she too is not smiling. The explanation of this is that her marriage took place in Pakistan, where brides are expected to look sad.

Statistically speaking, the marriages of both my great-great-grandmother and my niece were and are less likely to end in divorce than that of my daughter. Here we have some dramatic contrasts – times and places where marriage is not, for a woman at least, seen entirely as a joyful occasion, yet where the situation of divorce, should it occur, would be viewed as a total disaster for the woman concerned. By contrast, marriage in contemporary Britain is usually seen as a cause for celebration – certainly not a loss – but divorce has become common and is likely to bring very mixed feelings and responses for those concerned and from others. For example, it is possible now to buy 'congratulations on your divorce' cards – what does this tell us both about expectations and also about the ways in which such an event may be viewed?

Practice relevance

This section of the chapter has been designed to alert you to variations in the ways in which loss is defined. Although most of it concerns loss through death, and will be directly relevant to practice with people experiencing dying or bereavement, I hope that you can see that what is true of this extreme loss is also true of other situations with which we have to deal. For example, much social work with children is concerned with promoting or defending ideas of 'good enough parenting'. In some societies, a 'good parent' arranges for her daughter to be circumcised. In many societies, a good parent hits a child when he or she does not obey. When I lived in Pakistan, people did not usually explicitly deny anything to a young child (although not everything was in fact given) – I was considered harsh when I repeatedly said 'no' to my two year old. No wonder she had tantrums, I was told. Better by far to say 'yes' and then 'forget' or divert the child. As practitioners, we should be alert to such matters of cultural difference – see Robinson (2007) for a recent overview of issues in relation to child development in a cross cultural perspective. I mention them here to highlight the association with loss.

We grieve that which was expected or desired, and these matters vary across time and place. As expectations vary, so do our losses and how we understand them. Adoption is, for example, a situation that has many manifestations around the world, and that has been differently perceived and regulated over time.

A situation that dramatically highlights differences in the way in which loss may be defined or perceived is that that of disability. Sapey (2002) examines the objections put forward to an academic paper published by *Social Work Today* in 1988 that included the situation of disability within a discussion of 'traumatic' losses. Before looking at the arguments in more detail, the next activity asks you to consider your own response.

ACTIVITY **2.3**

Do you consider disability to be a form of loss?

Give reasons for your answer. Now look back at the definition of loss in Chapter 1. What, if any, distinctions would you wish to make?

Comment

You may have distinguished between loss from birth and loss which is acquired – in other words, between a situation where someone has lost some faculty that they previously had (such as their sight or hearing, or the use of a limb) and a situation where the person has not experienced any change. This would be consistent with the definition of loss as a change from a previous condition. However, I also said at the beginning of this section that loss might be the loss of something desired or expected, and referred to the loss that a parent may experience when a child is not 'perfect'. This raises a number of pertinent issues – such as 'from whose perspective is this loss?' You may recall that this question was also one asked in relation to the 'good death'. Those who argue for a social model of disability remind us that models of disability are not biologically self-evident, but reflect dominant or mainstream understandings of what it means to be 'normal'. This was powerfully brought home to me by a deaf social work student who told a class that he was glad that his baby had also been born deaf. His hearing mother (the baby's grandparent) saw this as a loss, however.

This issue, more than any other, illustrates the extent to which loss is itself socially defined and depends upon social understandings of what is desirable and normal. We will return to it later, in Chapter 4. In the next section, we look at the ways in which society also influences how we respond to loss.

Defining appropriate responses

Weinstein (2002) suggests that culture teaches us how to *think, feel* and *act* in the face of death, and that these understandings are often expressed in shared rituals. Barley (1995) makes the point that culture also dictates which of these is important – the emphasis upon authentic emotions and on beliefs *may simply be a largely Western obsession*. He continues:

> *In China great concern with common ritual response has gone quite happily with an overwhelming disregard for similarity of belief: it does not matter very much what you think you are doing as long as you do it like everyone else.* (1995, p10)

For a long time, there was an assumption that sadness and crying were universal responses to death and loss. But this is not the case. Self-mutilation by the bereaved is found in a number of societies and – at the other end of the spectrum – some societies forbid wailing or crying. Eisenbruch (1984) describes a variety of responses, and Wikan's (1988) paper comparing the loud wailing of mourners in Egypt with the smiling Balinese response gives a dramatic illustration from two particular societies.

Such evidence of variation augments our own experience. This may be of a contrast between two societies with which you are familiar or of change over time in relation to expectations of mourning. I can remember when people stopped by the roadside when a hearse passed, and doffed their hats or wore a black armband, for example. Clark (1993) describes rituals in Yorkshire in the early twentieth century. After a death, there are social expectations about (and even legal restrictions on) how a person will be commemorated (the funeral), how to dispose of the body and what memorials are appropriate or allowed. In addition, rituals and customs will cover people's expectations of the behaviour of others towards the bereaved. Because rituals and customs offer a useful lens on how a loss is perceived in society, we will start by defining the terms we use and then broaden our consideration to the rituals and customs that pertain (or do not pertain) in the case of other types of loss.

Rituals and customs

Customs and rituals have much in common with each other, although a ritual is more elaborate and formalised, often involving a series of customary practices. Some more precise definitions will be helpful at this point.

Customs are *established patterns of behaviour and belief* (Abercrombie et al., 1988, p59).

It is a custom, for example, in Western Europe, to have a pine tree indoors at Christmas time, and to decorate it. In various countries in Western Europe, there are differences in the decorations that are customary.

Rituals are *any formal actions following a set pattern which express through symbol a public or shared meaning* (Abercrombie et al., 1988, p209). Rituals are often explicitly religious, but they do not have to be. A church service is a ritual, but so is the opening of parliament, the opening ceremony of the Olympic Games, and even the Eurovision Song Contest.

Some rituals mark particular changes or transitions in the life cycle. These are known as 'rites of passage'. Rites of passage were first analysed by anthropologist Arnold van Gennep in the first decade of this century. Froggatt, who has applied these ideas to the modern hospice, writes of van Gennep's definition of rites of passage as *sets of customary behaviour that typically accompanied changes of place, state, social position and age.* (1997, p124). Coming of age ceremonies, marriage and funerals are important rites of passage. They may involve a number of different rituals and customs and take place over a period of time.

As we have seen, loss is closely tied up with change, so rites of passage may well be involved in at least some cases of loss. Before looking more closely at ways in which these notions have been applied recently, it is worth pausing to consider some of the customs and rituals familiar to us.

Marriage is significant in most societies. It signifies a change – in sociological terms, the setting up of a *family of procreation* and leaving the *family of origin* (Steel and Kidd, 2001, p15). The next activity asks you to think about the customs and rituals that surround this transition, both in your own culture and one other.

ACTIVITY **2.4**

Divide the page into three columns. In the first, make a list of all the customs that are for you associated with marriage. In the second column, do the same thing in respect of a culture that is not your own. Then in the third, note whether this is a custom or ritual, and what it concerns.

Customs and rituals associated with marriage

In the third column, you might have put 'customary clothes' or 'customary demeanour' and 'ritual before marriage'. Examples of clothes that are customary in England are a white dress for a bride and perhaps 'top hat and tails' for the groom. In Pakistan, the bride wears red. I have already referred to the customary demeanour of brides in my earlier discussion of 'the smiling bride'. You might have noted differences in religious ceremonies – one Christian, the other Muslim, for example. In Pakistan, there are rituals before the actual marriage. In England, we have 'stag' and 'hen' celebrations, which have changed significantly in recent years. A 'stag night' or party used to be held for the bridegroom and his young single friends on the night before the wedding, celebrating his last night of 'freedom'. He was leaving one social group, and the leisure activities associated with that group, for another state of being and a series of expectations. The bride-to-be was certainly not expected to be out partying at that time.

This example is one illustration of a number of different assumptions about the meaning of marriage and about gender roles. Many of these cultural assumptions – and their associated customs – have changed. Today, it seems often to be the case in Britain that both 'hen' and 'stag' nights are held (by both bride-to-be and groom, but separately); they have become more elaborate and are held some weeks or months earlier. This illustrates a number of social and cultural changes. It is probable now that the couple in this society are already living together before the ceremony; the significance of a 'last night' has changed for both parties. To some extent, this aspect of a 'rite of passage' has become 'detached', and changed in meaning. Changes also occur in relation to more formalised aspects of the rituals.

Customs and rituals marking other stages in the life course.

In Tikopia in the South Pacific, the loss of a tooth by a chief is traditionally an occasion for mourning by his family (Barley, 1995) as it signifies his ageing; in Britain, children put their first teeth under the pillow for the 'tooth fairy'. Customs are at their most transparent when we visit a culture that is not our own, because we do not immediately share the same expectations.

Rituals 'follow a set pattern', as we saw in the definition above. They may be individual acts (for example, a prayer time or service may only involve one person), but they do involve a sequence of events. Visiting the grave of someone who has died can involve a ritual for an individual, in which it is important to do things in a set order. Often, however, rituals involve more than one person – they are shared. Rituals have the character, because of the set pattern, of telling us what to do. The pattern may itself bring comfort, even for an individual. For example, on a bad day, a bereaved person may hardly feel able to go out. Yet the established pattern or sequence of events of needing to place flowers on a grave can 'take over'. As a result, they may go because this is 'what they do', and perhaps they will find this routine action comforting. This may also be the case in the ritual of the funeral. With the decline in accepted customs (such as wearing a black armband) and rituals following a death, many people complain that they do not know what to do. This can lead to embarrassment, and the bereaved person can feel very isolated, just at a time when they most need social support.

Rites of passage

Rites of passage marking a significant transition have a specific form which was described by van Gennep (1960 [1909]). They have three parts, which he called *separation*, *transition* and *incorporation*. In relation to rituals associated with death, this has been applied both to the person who has died, and to those who are bereaved. In the stage of separation, the person draws apart from others. This may well occur before death, or it may be marked by the funeral or disposal of the physical body. The bereaved person may also withdraw immediately after a death, for example, there may be time off work.

The period of transition has been called *limen* – a sort of half-way state. Many religions see the soul of the person who has recently died as lingering for a while after death (Gielen, 1997). The bereaved person may be in a parallel state – in Victorian times, there were rules which particularly governed the behaviour of widows in bereavement, and an early period of seclusion was expected, with no social calls. Turner (1969) has looked at the ritual process in detail, and this analysis has also been used to consider responses following a communal tragedy. This is a time when the usual social rules break down; those affected may behave as equals despite wide differences in social situation and status. Walter (1991) has looked at the way this happened after the Hillsborough disaster, and a similar process occurred following 9/11.

Depending upon your belief system, the dead person is 'received' amongst the dead – perhaps recognised as an ancestor in some cultures. The bereaved person re-enters social life after a time. This is the phase of *incorporation*. In some societies, there is a defined period of mourning, after which formal mourning is ended. For example, Jewish tradition separates out six graduated periods of mourning; *Sheloshim* being the name given to the period of 30 days after the funeral, which includes the seven days of *Shiva* that follow the burial (Levine, 1997). Such structured periods of mourning do not mean that the grief is over by a set time, but are to do with social observances that can facilitate that process.

Littlewood (1993) has brought together the work of various authors in considering what happens at the time of bereavement. She argues that in modern Western societies death and bereavement have become privatised and individualised; there has been a decline in ritual. This may reduce the social support available to a grieving person. If this is the case for death-related losses, it is even more marked in respect of other life transitions. Many significant life changes have no defined ceremonies or rites of passage. The next activity asks you to consider a situation in which there are few social markers.

ACTIVITY **2.5**

Consider the end of a marriage or relationship.

- *In your experience, what social customs mark this transition?*

- *At the time of a divorce, what do people do, and how does this represent what they are feeling?*

- *In your view, is the relative absence of customs at such a time a help or a hindrance to those involved?*

- *In what ways can the lack of social customs sometimes be a problem?*

The effects of an absence of customs or rituals

In British society, although divorce has become very common, there are few well-established rituals or customs to mark it. Some people hold a party when their 'decree' comes through the post; others may feel very miserable and stay at home and 'drown their sorrows'. Clearly this depends upon whether the end was one they themselves wanted, although most people have very mixed feelings at this time. Other people (if they are not very close friends) may not know whether to ring with congratulations or commiserations. Many people have spoken of the consequent loneliness they felt at the time of a very significant change that felt like a 'non-event' in social terms, but was hugely significant personally.

Overview: changing functions of customs and rituals

The commercial card market, and now the internet, have responded by suggesting ways to fill this gap – for example **www.healingdivorce.com** is one of a number of sites promoting the positive functions of 'do it yourself' rituals. This development represents an interesting reversal of tradition. Rituals and customs have traditionally reflected and affirmed shared belief systems. The newer rituals seem to offer collective ways of expressing personal truths, rather than personal ways of expressing shared ones. This too appears to be a reflection of the emphasis both on the individual and on feelings in postmodern society, and has come about because postmodern society has a distrust of any singular authority. Other collective expressions have arisen spontaneously – such as the habit of leaving flowers at the roadside site of an accident or the overwhelming response to the death of Diana, Princess of Wales.

Rosenblatt has the following comment:

> *Rituals may be understood in many different ways. Often a key to them seems to be that they define. They define the death, the cause of death, the dead person, the bereaved, the relationships of the bereaved with one another and with others, the meaning of life and other major societal values.* (Rosenblatt, 1997, p33)

We may wish to substitute 'loss' for death in this quotation.

For example, a funeral clearly defines that death has occurred. The cause of death is not always explicit, although it will be commonly referred to within the ritual or service, and funerals in which the cause or manner of death is mentioned may be more satisfying for the bereaved. For example, there may be an acknowledgement of long pain bravely borne, or of death's suddenness and the lack of time to say goodbye. In some cases, defining the cause of death is difficult, and the formal inquest becomes the public venue in which this definition occurs. Defining the cause of death may be enormously significant for bereaved people. The inquest (and even maybe a later public enquiry) then almost becomes a part of the overall ritual. A definition of the bereaved and of their relationships with each other can be very apparent at a funeral – who is the 'main mourner' for example? Where do people sit? Who is excluded? This relates back to the discussion in Chapter 1 of 'disenfranchised grief'. A lover may not be aware of the date of a funeral, let alone be invited. Children or those with a learning disability may not be included in rituals. This is a definition of their status.

So we are back to meaning as a crucial factor. Socially, rituals express and affirm shared meanings. Life changes and transitions are often times when the meaning of life has to be redefined. For example, after the birth of a child, life has to be redefined as a parent. The physical presence of a baby needing attention forces practical changes; there are also changes in terms of how the parents view themselves. After a stillbirth, we see an example where status has changed, but practicalities have not. Yet the change has occurred; the meaning of life has changed, not only because the person is now a parent, but also because they have experienced a significant and traumatic loss.

The social regulation of grief

Social expectations about appropriate grieving behaviour do not just offer a range of actions from which we can choose on an individual basis, although the postmodern climate is one in which this may be seen as an ideal. They are part and parcel of social expectations about how we should and should not behave. These social expectations are the basis of a famous novel by existentialist writer Albert Camus. The central character is his novel *The Outsider* (1982 [1942]) is a man who does not grieve for his mother's death in ways that are expected. This man is ostracised and eventually executed as a consequence of his lack of regard for social conventions. In most cases, the consequences are not so extreme, but the expectations are very real, nonetheless! Rosenblatt comments:

> *I know of no society in which the emotions of bereavement are not shaped and controlled, for the sake of the deceased, the bereaved person, or others.* (Rosenblatt, 1997, p36)

We will look separately at how grieving is regulated or 'policed' at the individual and political levels, and also at collective responses to grief that demonstrate and express solidarity.

Social regulation at the individual level

This happens through the giving of advice, or praising those who behave well. In some societies, where there is a high level of overt consensus and a strong system of authority, these expectations are very explicit. Victorian society was one in which there were clearly laid down expectations in relation to mourning, particularly for widows. Black was to be worn initially, and then lilac. A young widow could not be seen in public until after a proscribed length of time. In a society such as Britain's today, however, there is less social consensus or agreement about the right way to behave, and advice may be contradictory. Consider this comment by a young widow:

> *When I slowly started to enjoy life again, and looked happy, it was rumoured that I couldn't be missing Ian all that much, but on the occasions when I was sad and depressed, I was told to stop being so miserable.* (Stuart, 1994)

There is a gendered aspect to such regulation also.

Walter sees social work as allied to the 'psi-sciences' whose function is, in part, to regulate grieving. He argues that a new cadre of experts has arisen in the form of bereavement counsellors. As experts, part of their social function is to guide others in how to grieve properly. Through articles in popular magazines and even soap operas, these messages become generally absorbed by all of us. But we are all involved in the informal policing of grief in subtle ways through the expectations we have of others.

The next exercise asks you to think about your own family.

Consider your own family, and think about the rules, roles and expectations that surround death.

What rules are there about what can and cannot be discussed in your family? What are the expectations concerning social behaviour at times of crisis or loss?

Finally, how are roles distributed? Is there one person who is the one everyone talks to? One person who acts as a channel for communication? What happens or would happen if they were gone? Is gender a feature of these expectations?

Comment

In one family, a certain aunt was the person who always passed on the gossip – when she died, it took everyone some time to realise why they felt so cut off from each other. New roles had to be established. If your family is one that is separated by distance, you will have experienced the difficulties that arise when certain members are not present or close enough. In some situations there may be different expectations for someone in their country of origin and in the place where they now live. Clearly, your answers will be individual, but this activity is included to encourage you to realise that social regulation is not just something that others do – it is an integral feature of social life for us all.

Social regulation at the level of society

In sociological terms, grief is a potential threat to society because, like illness, it threatens work and family life – society could not continue if we all took too much time off for bereavement, or if everything stopped – so there must be various rules about how to behave. These are enshrined in social policy – in how much time is allowed off work, for example. Social policy also endorses certain losses or life changes as ones that require support or intervention, whilst others are ignored. An example might be the development of specialist private and charitable support services to help 'traumatised children' displaying challenging behaviour (Lepper, 2007). The author of this particular article refers to the fact that access to specialist services for traumatised children has been ignored by the government. Hospice provision – although recognised and endorsed publicly – remains largely funded by local charities. Through what is financed and promoted, and through services that are sidelined or neglected, governments give messages about what is important within society.

Goss and Klass (2005) offer striking examples of the ways in which political regimes have suppressed or encouraged certain grief rituals at times of change – for example, in China, ancestor worship and the use of family shrines were forbidden at the time of the Cultural Revolution, and new rituals were adopted in which work colleagues were seen as the main mourners. This illustrates well the way in which rituals define appropriate behaviour.

Collective action and support

Goss and Klass (2005) are concerned with tracing the ways in which people maintain continuing bonds with those who have died. They also identify the present day as a time when grieving has become difficult because of the cultural emphasis on individual autonomy in Western societies. They argue that grieving has become privatised, saying that *when grief is conceptualised as a psychological process, it is painful, but ultimately not meaningful.* (Goss and Klass, 2005, p256). They are therefore interested in the ways in which people seek solidarity in grief, and find these in the new rituals that have emerged almost 'spontaneously' (such as flowers by the site of a roadside accident). We could perhaps add the ways of communicating following a loss that have been made possible through the internet. For example, the charity Winston's Wish (**www.winstons wish.org.uk**) has set up a skyscape of memories – an interactive featureboard on which bereaved children can place their own pictures and messages. Goss and Klass (2005) point to the development of self-help groups, and also describe the creation of the 'AIDS quilt', which was a powerful means by which gay people celebrated their dead partners collectively – creating a memorial which was collective and which symbolises connection rather than individuality. They argue that

> Grieving is an inter-subjective process, not just a psychological process. Grieving, then is not about autonomy .... Grief is about participation in community. (Goss and Klass, 2005, p276)

Lessons for social work

So what relevance does all this have for social work practice? I have identified the following, but you may have thought of others as you went through the chapter.

- Factors such as gender and culture powerfully affect our understanding both of what counts as loss and of what should be done about it. This means that any work with a service user must seek to identify their expectations and unspoken assumptions.

- When you are working with someone who is visibly different from yourself, because they are from a different cultural or racial background, you may be alerted to the impact of social issues. Yet these are important for all of us, and we should not assume that we share a common view without checking this out. Whilst this may be especially important if your service user is of a different ethnicity, age, or gender, it is always good practice.

- You need to be aware of the fact that behaviour and even emotion are socially regulated – who is exerting pressure on the person you are working with to behave in a certain way? This pressure may come from their own internalised 'policing' or expectations as much as from actual people around them.

- Such pressure may be helpful or unhelpful for the person concerned; it may be accompanied by support – or by support which is conditional on 'correct behaviour'. Understanding these social pressures may be a means to give the service user the choice of deciding which 'voices' they will comply with, or how to deal with the expectations placed upon them by others.

47

- It has been suggested (Holloway, 2007b) that an attention to religious beliefs and spiritual need can be problematic for social workers – yet these issues are important ones when we are working with loss because they concern meaning.

- When you are working with someone who has a defined religious belief, remember that their personal belief system may well not be in line with a public expression of faith, but is likely to be negotiated within these understandings, and may borrow from other ways of seeing the issue that lie outside the orthodox religious framework.

- What customs and rituals are available to the person you are working with in relation to the loss they are experiencing? If none exist, could they be created?

- We have looked at the ways in which social policy also defines and regulates at a social level. This may have an impact through actions that are permitted or possible and others that are not.

I have tried to show that social customs and social relations can offer a framework of support for the individual as well as a system of control. We are social beings, and as Goss and Klass argue, social action and solidarity can offer means of counteracting the isolation that pain and grief can bring. At times of communal tragedy or disaster, social barriers seem to break down as people share their grief with strangers. It is easy to see meaning making in very individual terms, but meaning has to be created socially for it to offer a secure basis for the individual. In this individualised, postmodern society, where the most popular funeral tune is *(I Did It) My Way*, there is a need for attention to be paid in both theory and practice to the support that can be offered through shared meanings, and expressions of them.

C H A P T E R   S U M M A R Y

This chapter has sought to counteract the common tendency to view loss as an individual experience by considering the ways in which society defines what is considered to be a loss and how we express grief and expect others to behave. This perspective is important for the practitioner, because it forms the basis of practice which is truly anti-discriminatory by creating the ability to see the pain and grief experienced by individuals against a broader canvass. The tendency to focus upon death-related loss has been particularly marked in this chapter, because much of the theoretical debate – from subjects such as sociology and anthropology – has this focus. However, I have tried, through a variety of activities, to encourage you to consider other situations, such as those relating to marriage and divorce.

Whilst we are all constrained by social norms and customs, these also offer powerful support – not least at times of crisis and loss. There are differences between societies and also within societies in the extent of support that individuals may expect in their loss. Those who are cut off from their cultural roots or social systems may therefore find themselves doubly disadvantaged at times of loss, because the social supports normally available or expected may not be accessible to them. Whilst this may apply following migration particularly, it may also be the case where a person finds themselves removed from expected forms of social support for other reasons – such as in old age, for example, when peers have died and an individual may feel themselves to be alienated by a culture in which the old rules no longer apply.

We will turn in the next chapters to look at models and theories of grieving which have a more individual focus. The ideas explored in this chapter form a backdrop for this.

Holloway, M (2007a) *Negotiating death in contemporary health and social care*. Bristol: Policy Press.

This book is highly recommended. It offers a comprehensive overview for practitioners of the ways in which death is regulated and understood, including questions and practice scenarios that show the relevance of the issues to contemporary health and social care.

Parkes, CM, Laungani, P and Young, B (eds) (1997) *Death and bereavement across cultures*. London: Routledge.

Contains chapters outlining cultural customs in a number of different societies and religious groups. A useful source.

Field, D, Hockey, J and Small, N (eds) (1997) *Death, gender and ethnicity*. London: Routledge.

This collection considers the extent to which gender and ethnicity influence dying and bereavement with examples from a range of different settings. It has a sociological rather than anthropological basis, with rather more of a critical edge.

Hockey, J, Katz, J and Small, N (eds) (2001) *Grief, mourning and death ritual*. Buckingham: Open University Press.

Another edited collection, but with a broad focus and some chapters with direct relevance to social care.

Marris, P (1991) The social construction of uncertainty, in Parkes, C. et al. (eds), *Attachment across the life cycle*. London: Routledge.

This is a single chapter, that looks at loss and uncertainly more broadly – making a case for linking attachment theory with a sociological perspective.

Chapter 3
Experiencing loss: models and theories

Introduction

In this chapter, and the next, we look at the various ways in which responses to loss have been described and classified, and the 'models' that have resulted from such classifications. These models – with their underlying theories about the nature of grief and grieving – have had a powerful influence upon practice in all the human service occupations such as social work, nursing, medicine and counselling. Many have had their roots in practice in these helping professions, so we should not be surprised to find this close link.

Response to loss involves both letting go of the past and continuity with it. The theme of letting go of the past, together with a pattern of emotional responses associated with this letting go, has dominated early theories. Social and cultural differences, such as those which were the focus of the last chapter, have not been evident in early theories and models. Yet these models and understandings remain important for us as practitioners. This is partly because they remain very influential – through practitioners who were training when they represented the 'received wisdom' and because they have been passed on to and adopted by the general public. It is also because they still represent one aspect of the experience of grieving – one strand in a grieving process that we now see as more nuanced and variable. In the next chapter, we will take this exploration of models further, looking at particular features of loss in childhood and old age, at ambiguous loss and at the concept of resilience. We start now, however, by thinking about the responses we have following the loss of an object.

Responses to everyday losses

The loss of an object

We can learn quite a lot about our responses to loss by imagining the simple situation of losing an object that has significance for us. Of course, there are important differences between the loss of a thing and the loss of a person we love – whether through death or some other reason – and we will pay attention to these as we go through the chapter, but for now let us start just by noting our own responses to the loss of an object. The first activity in this chapter asks you to imagine your own responses when you lose an object that is important to you. This activity asks you to engage in imaginative reflection – you should try this when you can be in a quiet place for 15 minutes, and if you can enlist the help of a friend, this would also be beneficial. Have a pen and paper close at hand, and sit somewhere that you feel comfortable. If a friend can help you with the activity, ask them to read the instructions to you, pausing at the appropriate places. If you are alone, read this through once, just to see what you have to do, but try not to pre-empt your responses.

ACTIVITY 3.1

Think of an object that is precious to you. This might be a piece of jewellery, for example. The activity works best if it is something that is precious for emotional rather than simply practical reasons. Then make yourself comfortable. You are going to imagine that the object is lost, and there are four stages. Each stage involves a short time of quiet, when you will close your eyes and try to picture yourself in the situation described, followed by jotting down some words that describe your feelings. If a friend is helping, they could give you a set time of – say – 60 seconds for imagining a stage, and then tell you when each one is over.

1. Shut your eyes and imagine the moment when you have just discovered the loss of this object. Try to get into the situation in your imagination; smell the smells, experience the sensations. What are you feeling? Stay with this for as long as it is working for you,

> ### ACTIVITY 3.1 *continued*
>
> or until your friend tells you to stop, then open your eyes and write down the words that describe your feelings.
>
> 2. Repeat – it is now two hours later.
>
> 3. Repeat – it is now a week later.
>
> 4. Repeat – it is now a year later.

Responses to losing an object

Some people find it easier to engage in this type of imaginative exercise than others. Don't worry if you found it hard to get into the situation. On the other hand, if it was fairly easy, and the situation seemed very real, you may want to go and reassure yourself that the precious object you pictured is where you think it is!

Here are some of the responses to this activity from social work students.

Moment of loss	Two hours later	A week later	A year later
Confused	Empty	Apathy	Acceptance
Denial	Fearful	Despair	Still angry
Disbelieving	Searching	Still hoping	Replacing it
Anxious	Isolated	Sadness	Forgotten, but memory can be triggered
Panicked	Sad	Emptiness in stomach	Extra careful
Frustrated	Guilty	Beginning to accept it is lost	Resigned
Tearful	Stressed	Guilty	'Nothing can replace it'
Hot flush	Panting	Flashbacks	Very sad when I remember
Irrational	Talking to self	Resignation	Over-protective
'Hyper'	Angry/furious	Dreaming of finding it	Wiser
Accusing	Tearful/upset	Tranquillisers or alcohol	
Angry with self	Hopeful	Avoiding thinking about it	
Numb	Preoccupied	Planning to replace	
Desolated	Stupid	Feeling a failure	
Sick	More frantic		
	Still looking		
	Obsessive		
	Rationalising		
	Having a drink		
	Blaming self		

I wonder how your own responses compare with these lists. If you look at these responses, you will notice that some feelings occur in more than one list, and also that some physical sensations such as feeling sick or empty have been noted.

Losing a person

Feelings

Comparing the students' list with those to be found in sources that list the manifestations of normal grief following bereavement, (e.g. Worden, 1991, pp22–30; Payne et al., 1999, pp23–4), the feelings commonly noted are mostly covered in the list above. These sources add in such factors as:

- a feeling of fatigue;

- helplessness;

- shock;

- yearning;

and sometimes also

- relief or a sense of emancipation.

Physical sensations

If we consider physical sensations that commonly accompany grief, we find, in addition to an 'emptiness in the stomach' that people also report the following:

- tightness in the chest or throat;

- over-sensitivity to noise;

- breathlessness;

- weakness in the muscles;

- a dry mouth;

- a lack of energy;

- 'depersonalisation' (this is the sensation of feeling that you are unreal).

Cognitions

In terms of what have been called 'disorders of thinking', you may notice that the student responses refer to disbelief, confusion and obsessive thinking. These are common in the early stages of grief, with the following additions noted in the literature:

- self-doubt (which is close to guilt, but not the same);

- hallucinations;

- a sense of the person who has died being present.

A sense of the dead person's presence is a very common sensation, which was picked up in early studies as culturally variable, being reported in 90% of cases in one small study in Japan (Yamamoto et al., 1969), compared with 39% in another study in Wales (Rees, 1971). As we will see, such perceptions link with theories about grief which emphasise the continuation of a bond. In such a framework, we might wish to query the idea that this represents 'disordered' thinking. For now, we will just note that it is one of the common responses that people have.

Behavioural changes

These thoughts and feelings are linked to altered behaviours for many people. In addition to the dreams, searching and avoiding reminders (all noted by students following the activity above), there may be:

- disturbances of sleep and appetite;
- absent-mindedness;
- social withdrawal;
- repeated sighing;
- restless over-activity;
- or visiting of places and treasuring objects that were associated with to the person who has gone.

What do we learn from all this? The activity concerned only the loss of an object, but there are clearly commonalties with feelings, thoughts and behaviours following the death of someone special. Although the loss of a person is not the same as the loss of an object, there are some similarities in the effects.

Marris warns us against seeing too great a similarity, saying that:

> *losing someone you love is less like losing a very valuable and irreplaceable possession than like finding the law of gravity to be invalid.* (Marris, 1982)

He is reminding us here that despite superficial similarities in the way that we may respond emotionally and physically, a close bereavement has a more profound effect, in necessitating a revision of all that we believed to be true. It threatens not only our bodies, but our very *ontological security* (Giddens, 1991) or sense of being safe in the world. We will return to this point below.

Despite this caution that grief is more than a sum of symptoms, the sensations themselves can be very alarming for someone who is grieving, and it is important that practitioners are aware that a wide range of feelings and other responses is quite normal. This can be very reassuring, provided it is not used to dismiss the feelings that someone is experiencing. For example, anger is a common response to grief – much unnecessary suffering would be avoided if this were known and taken seriously by those working in day centres for people with learning difficulties. Too often normal responses to a death are misinterpreted as being due to the learning difficulty rather than to grief (Oswin, 1990).

It is time now to look at the various models or frameworks that have been used to describe and categorise grief reactions, before turning to consider the theoretical assumptions and ideas that are reflected in these descriptions. Many – but not all – concern death-related losses.

Grief in literature

Literature is full of portrayals of the response to loss, and this is fertile ground for anyone seeking to understand grief. The study of grief and loss is, in this sense, as old as human history, and found in all cultures. Weinstein (2002) advocates the use of literature by students training for social work as a means to understanding loss, and you may already have your own favourites – either from the classics or contemporary film or literature. In case you don't know where to start, see Hammick (1992) for a collection of short stories on the theme of love and loss, and Gersie (1991) for cross cultural examples of story making in bereavement. We also have first-hand accounts of both dying and bereavement such as that by Ruth Picardie (1998), who died of cancer, and Oscar Moore (1996) who wrote about his dying from AIDS. CS Lewis's personal account of his own bereavement (1961) became the film *Shadowlands* (Attenborough and Eastman, 1993), and the film *Iris* (Eyre and Wood, 2001) offered a portrayal of the profound losses caused by Alzheimer's disease. Such accounts have been drawn upon by practitioners seeking to understand the experience of loss from a first-hand perspective – for example, Currer (2001) analyses some themes from Picardie and Moore's accounts, whilst Attig (2002) has based a recent review on that of Lewis. We turn now to look at the ways in which loss and grief have been described, classified and understood within the scientific and social science literature.

Descriptions and early models

Classifications and models of grief responses

In twentieth century Western society, grief has been studied from a more detached perspective, although this shares with the accounts in literature the detailed observation of individual responses. The models of grieving that have gained in popularity have usually been based on research in practice settings. Understanding grief and loss has been associated for some while with the work of two very influential practitioners – Elisabeth Kübler-Ross (1926–2004), who studied the responses of people in the USA following a terminal diagnosis, and Colin Murray Parkes, an English psychiatrist whose life work concerns bereavement and loss, and the links that such events do and do not have with mental illness. Influential as these people have been, they were not the first to note and categorise the responses that people experience when they are grieving.

There are various reviews in the literature of grieving models (see, for example, Payne et al., 1999; Currer, 2001; Small, 2001; Thompson, 2002a; Hooyman and Kramer, 2006, for some recent examples). Here, I have chosen to introduce these models in relation to the situations on which the research was based. Not all concern death-related situations, although many do. The research base is important because we cannot assume without question that grief is either universal or follows the same pattern whatever its cause. If our interest were only in grief following death, this would be less of an issue since this is the situation that has given rise to many of the models, or in relation to which they have mainly been tested. As social workers, we will all meet people who are coping with situations of dying and bereavement (Currer, 2001), despite the common perception that such work is for specialist settings only. But what we are also interested in here – in common with Thompson (2002b) – is to explore the extent to which models of grief are applicable to a much broader range of losses. This issue was raised in Chapter 1, when we noted that losses themselves vary in respect of a number of features which can themselves be delineated, and also looked at ways of classifying loss.

The models that are outlined in this section relate, then, to different types of loss. They also reflect different theoretical assumptions about the nature of grief and loss. These underlying approaches – psychodynamic theories; attachment theory; theories of stress, crisis and coping; constructivism – will be considered later in this chapter.

Responses following a catastrophic fire

Lindemann (1994 [1944]) interviewed bereaved relatives in two main studies – one concerned servicemen killed in the Second World War, the other those who died following a catastrophic nightclub fire. Based upon this research and his clinical experience his work followed that of Freud, who in 1917 had identified aspects of so called 'normal' and 'abnormal' grief. Some of the factors that Lindemann noticed – such as a preoccupation with images of the person who died, guilt, anger and somatic (physical) disturbances – feature in later models, and in the responses that have already been noted. He also used the term 'anticipatory grief' to describe aspects of the reaction of women who feared that their husbands would die fighting in World War II.

As we saw in the last chapter, cultural aspects of grieving have been slow to be recognised. A rarely cited but notable paper by Ablon (1986 [1973]) studied the reactions of Samoan people living in America to a later but similar fire in which many members of the close-knit Samoan community were killed. The response of the Samoans to uncertainty, trauma and bereavement was described by many of the doctors and emergency personnel as 'stoical'. Ablon compared these responses to those described in Lindemann's earlier research, and found that there were significant differences in response. Three factors were seen as influential as contributing to the Samoan's calm approach and lack of panic: social position, group support and religion. I have already described this community as 'close-knit' – the social support available included practical matters such as childcare by other community members for those who went to the hospital to sit by a bedside or identify a body. The Samoans were devout Christians and saw this as influencing their responses, but they also referred to the fact that they were used to working hard to survive and that they had no expectation of immediate help – in contrast to white Americans, who became angry when ambulances were delayed, for example.

These, then, were situations of sudden and traumatic loss, and bereavement was the focus of both studies, as well as responses to crisis and trauma.

Children separated from their primary caregivers

John Bowlby's seminal work on loss and grief (1969, 1973, 1980) was influenced by investigations into the reactions of young children who had been separated from their mothers. Studies of the effects of maternal deprivation, and the work of James Robertson who studied and later filmed the reactions of young children separated from their primary caregivers, were both influences leading to Bowlby's development of Attachment Theory, which has become enormously influential within social work (Howe, 1995). We will consider this more fully below. The roots of this body of work were not initially death-related losses, therefore, but temporary separation, and the research subjects were young children, including those in institutional care. In relation to children separated from their caregivers, three phases of 'protest', 'despair' and 'detachment' were noted.

Bowlby and colleagues noticed that the responses of adults following the death of a partner were very much like these responses of young children, and this led to a version of the 'phases of grief' (Bowlby and Parkes, 1970) amplified by the addition of an initial phase of numbness that had been apparent in Parkes's study of widows. These phases appeared in Bowlby's third volume (1971) and they quickly became popular, but were also used to describe and guide so-called 'normal grief', which had not been the authors' intention (Parkes, 2006).

RESEARCH SUMMARY

Phases of Grief

- **Numbness** *(Bowlby and Parkes, 1970)* or **shock and denial** *(Bowlby, 1971).*

- **Yearning and protest**, *with associated anger and often searching.*

- **Despair.**

- **Gradual recovery.**

(Bowlby and Parkes, 1970, and Bowlby, 1971)

Later studies have used this work to look at the part played in responses to loss both by early attachment patterns and also at attachment as itself the basic mechanism at work in loss situations, whether of children or adults, and in relation both to death and other situations of loss. See, for example, Howe et al. (1992) on the responses of birth mothers following the loss of a child through adoption; Jewett (1984) on children's responses to fostering and adoption; and Kroll (1994, 2002) on the responses of children on their separation from a parent in situations of separation and divorce. Here is an example from Howe et al's (1992) study of birth mothers.

RESEARCH SUMMARY

The feelings of birth mothers

Howe et al. (1992) *note that the responses of women who have given up babies for adoption illustrate many of those described following bereavement, specifically:*

1. *Shock and immediate loss: 'I handed over the child, I've blacked out exactly what happened'; 'I couldn't concentrate at all'.*

2. *Yearning, searching and misery: 'I found myself looking at babies in the street wondering if they were my daughter all the time'.*

3. *Anger and feelings of both helplessness and hopelessness:*

   'But after a while, instead of crying, I seemed to be screaming all the time. I was so mad, so angry ...'

4. *Guilt: 'I still have so much guilt; I gave away my own baby. I know I was very young and there were so many very good reasons but ...'*

5. *Depression, despair and unresolved grief: 'I still feel as if a part of me is missing. I feel incomplete'. 'There's hardly a day goes by without me thinking of her'.*

What serious losses have in common: psychosocial transitions

Parkes (1996) was interested in clarifying any similarities or differences that might exist between the loss of a person and other losses. He therefore looked at both the loss of a limb and the loss of a home. The findings showed remarkable similarities with the responses to bereavement that had been previously described.

RESEARCH SUMMARY

Parkes's amputee study

Parkes identified seven features which he saw as major aspects of bereavement reactions. He then looked at the extent to which these were present in amputees. They were:

1. *A process of denial – all experienced a 'phantom limb'; this was a psychological as well as a physiological response.*

2. *Alarm, anxiety and restlessness were common.*

3. *A searching reaction is more complicated, but he observed amputees pining for their previous ability to run, swim etc. as they had before the amputation.*

4. *Anger, bitterness and guilt were present, together with envy of others.*

5. *Feelings of internal loss and mutilation of the self extended beyond the limb to the whole person.*

6. *Bereaved people often seemed to identify with the loved one who was gone; a parallel reaction was related to an identification with the lost limb, treating the phantom limb as an ongoing part of the self. As for the bereaved, this initial response usually disappeared with time, but for a few, it persisted.*

7. *The so-called 'pathological variants of grief' – which might be prolonged, excessive or inhibited – were also observed in those who had lost a limb.*

In his study of relocation, each of these components was again found to be present. Feelings of bodily mutilation were expressed as metaphors such as 'I felt like my heart was taken out of me'. (Parkes, 1996)

One of the important things to emerge from this further work was Parkes's theory of psycho-social transitions. In comparing losses of different kinds, and realising that attachment theory could not account for those that did not involve a primary relationship, however similar the responses seemed to be in practical terms, Parkes asked what it is that makes some losses particularly difficult. This led him to speak of the 'assumptive world' which is that aspect of the way in which we see the world that we assume to be true, and which we take for granted – until it is threatened by loss. This includes aspects of our identity, but also assumptions about our ability to cope with danger, and about how others will respond. This recognition of the importance of the ways in which we think about life and about ourselves is a feature of many of the more recent understandings of loss and grief that will be considered later in this chapter. It draws our attention not just to the emotional responses that we may have following a loss, but to the cognitive work of reconstructing our mental models following a major loss.

RESEARCH SUMMARY

Psycho-social transitions

What makes some losses particularly difficult?

The kinds of losses that bring about profound changes to the social environment of the individual. Parkes calls these psycho-social transitions *and defines them as follows:*

Psycho-social transitions:

1. require people to undertake a major revision of their assumptions of the world;

2. are lasting in their implications rather than transient;

3. take place over a relatively short time, so there is little opportunity for preparation.

(Parkes, 1971)

Peter Marris, a sociologist, also studied the loss of a home through looking at relocation – a change that was designed to be positive. In his (1986) analysis of loss and change, he noted an aspect similar to that commented on by Parkes. Marris called this *structures of meaning*, which he defines as *the organised structures of understanding and emotional attachments by which grown people interpret and assimilate their environment* (Marris, 1986, p4). He argued that human beings have an inbuilt conservative impulse – a bias towards predictability that brings a resistance to change. Grief results from the necessity to change and the consequent need to revise our assumptions about the world. Loss and change affect our ability to control our environment and therefore they provoke anxiety.

The work of Parkes and Marris takes us into a broader consideration of theory and of the ways in which grief is to be understood. This is a subject we will look at later in this chapter, but first we need to complete the review of models of grief by outlining one of the most influential – that of Elisabeth Kübler-Ross.

Responding to a terminal diagnosis

As with the work of Lindemann and of Bowlby, that of Kübler-Ross was based on observations in or related to a clinical environment. Here the basis was not trauma and bereavement, as for Lindemann, or infant separation, as for Bowlby, but the breaking of bad news – the diagnosis of a terminal illness. Her famous stages were originally (1970) stages of dying, but have also been called 'the five stages of grief' (Kübler-Ross and Kessler, 2005).

RESEARCH SUMMARY

Kübler-Ross's Stages

- **Denial:** *this is a very common initial reaction to bad news – 'it can't be true'. Sometimes it is more elaborate. Kübler-Ross cites a woman who insisted that her X-rays had been muddled with someone else's. In relation to bereavement, she suggests that many people will not accept the person has died until they see their body.*

RESEARCH SUMMARY *continued*

- *Anger:* *'Why me?'* *This rage may be directed against God, the professionals or family members. Someone must be blamed. Bereaved people may be angry to be left behind or at the manner of the person's death.*

- *Bargaining:* *Kübler-Ross describes the 'deals' that people make with fate, for example, to stay alive (or to hold it together) until after the birth of a grandchild or a family wedding.*

- *Depression:* *this marks the beginning of acceptance, there may be guilt and a sense of unworthiness as well as sadness.*

- *Acceptance:* *this may not be a contented or happy stage, but does represent the end of the struggle. For the bereaved, she suggests it is about learning to live with it.*

(Kübler-Ross, 1970; Kübler-Ross and Kessler, 2005)

Whilst Kübler-Ross's books give illustrations both from the situation of the dying person themself and of relatives following bereavement, we do need to exercise a little caution. Facing my own death clearly differs in some respects to responding following the death of someone I care about, however similar the emotional response may appear to be. One is a loss that concerns myself; the other concerns someone else. In one case the event has yet to happen; in the other it has already occurred. Despite this and other criticisms of these stages (see Corr, 1993; Thompson, 2002a, p3), this model has been one of the most influential for practitioners in all fields, from nursing to management studies – and in relation to many different losses.

Regarding the response to a terminal diagnosis, there has been further work and an alternative, more flexible, framework put forward by Buckman (1998; see also Currer, 2001, p40). There has also been further exploration of the concept of denial (see Sheldon, 1997, pp62–4), distinguishing disagreement with the diagnosis from unconscious processes and looking at ways of working with this. These are all considerable advances upon the basic model, and if your work is with people who are dying or receiving bad news, you should look at these alternatives rather than relying on the original model. Yet it continues to be very influential, and it is important therefore that you are familiar with it.

Reflection – commonalities and problems

Before moving on to look at modifications of these models and critiques of them, let us pause for a moment to review the material outlined so far. The next activity asks you to look back and identify what the various models outlined so far have in common.

ACTIVITY **3.2**

Look back over this chapter and at your responses to Activity 3.1 and the list of responses on page 52. Now look at the models of Bowlby and Kübler-Ross. What features do they have in common?

Comment

I expect that you will have noticed that the models are very similar overall, despite their different roots. You may have found that they are quite familiar. It is probably because they are close to many peoples' experience that they have become so popular. This popularity has led to them being used in ways their authors never intended (Kübler-Ross and Kessler, 2005; Parkes, 2006), as rigid frameworks through which people are expected to pass when they experience loss. For example, a worker might comment that 'she should be moving out of denial by now', or dismiss a reasonable complaint on the basis that the patient was angry and because it is a 'normal' response, rather than because something had indeed been done wrong.

There is also an assumption of progression and there was an early expectation that the phases or stages were in a fixed sequence, and that everyone passed through them all in order. This can make it sound very deterministic and passive. In response to this, William Worden (1991), who was interested in using this work in mental health settings with bereaved adults, developed the idea of 'tasks of mourning'. Instead of seeing these responses as phases that a person would move through, Worden developed tasks which could then become the counselling goals. He suggested a sequence of four tasks for the bereaved adult, as follows:

RESEARCH SUMMARY

Worden's Tasks of Mourning

1. ***To accept the reality of the loss.*** *The task here is to go over the event, in order to help the reality of it to sink in. This task can be seen in some ways as counteracting the tendency initially to shock and denial of what has occurred.*

2. ***To work through the pain of grief.*** *This is about expressing rather than repressing the feelings associated with the loss, and is seen to be essential. The feelings experienced may encompass all those described elsewhere; anger as well as sadness, guilt or powerlessness.*

3. ***To adjust to an environment in which the deceased is missing.*** *This is about the implications of the bereavement, which may be practical as well as emotional.*

4. ***To emotionally relocate the deceased and move on with life.***

The original (1983) version of this task was:

4. **To withdraw energy from the past and reinvest in other relationships.**

Worden altered the wording of his tasks in the later (1991) edition of his book following criticisms of early models, including of his own tasks of mourning. The most significant alteration was to the fourth and final task, and the revision that he made gives you an indication of one of the criticisms. The language of withdrawing energy from past relationships derives from the ideas of Freud, as we shall see. It suggests a leaving behind of the person who has died, which is not the experience of many people following bereavement. Rather, the relationship continues, and there is a process of readjustment or 'relocation' that has to take place.

Criticisms of these models – or perhaps of the use made of them – gathered momentum in the 1990s, and we turn to consider these next.

Critique and more recent understandings

Is there a 'right way' to grieve?

Because the models seemed to indicate a 'right way' to grieve, an associated literature developed concerned with 'pathological grief' – the wrong ways to grieve. Look at the following definition of 'pathological grief':

> *Pathological grief is a deviation from the norm (i.e. the grieving reaction that could be expected, given the extremity of the particular bereavement event) in the time span or in the intensity of specific or general symptoms of grief. Subtypes have been identified as chronic, delayed or absent grief.* (Stroebe et al., 1998)

For most social workers the term 'pathological' suggests a medical model, and it is now more common to speak of *complicated grief* (Parkes, 2006), although this may still be clinically measured and conceived.

However much we may dislike any such classifications (and most people now emphasise that grieving is individual and unique), we are likely to meet with people who are themselves wishing to change their responses or to find some relief and ways of moving forward. The following example illustrates the issue.

CASE STUDY

Tina and Joe had three young daughters. They lived in a three-bedroomed house, and the two youngest girls shared a bedroom. When their eldest child Samantha died in a road accident, Tina could not bear to alter her bedroom, and kept it just as it was when she left it – with all her toys in place. Four years later and the birth of a baby boy brought pressure to change. For the rest of the family, there was an obvious solution, but not for Tina. The rows over this were making everyone in the family miserable. Although she could see that they were right, any change was too threatening for her. She agreed to seek help from a bereavement counsellor.

There are also occasions when a person may destroy their own life through a fixation on their difficulties. Another example illustrates this point.

CASE STUDY

Jack had lost the use of his legs in an accident, and was now confined to a wheelchair. At the time of the accident, his wife and children were very supportive and tried to encourage him to make a new life and to enjoy the hobbies that he could still pursue. Sadly, Jack became obsessed with what he had lost and would speak of little else. His wife left him and his children now rarely saw him. He lived in a residential unit where other residents (as well as staff) were also tired of his attitude and lack of interest in anyone else's problems or conversation.

For Jack, there may have been an earlier point at which skilled help would have enabled him to make choices that gave him a better future. There may also be a need to distinguish a grief reaction from a depression that needs to be referred to mental health specialists. In these earlier models of grieving, so-called 'pathological grief' was defined in relation to a 'norm' in terms of time and intensity. In these terms, both Tina's and Jack's grief reactions may well have been classified by others as 'pathological'. Perhaps a more helpful question is not 'Is this normal?' but rather 'Is this response threatening other aspects of life, such as social relationships?' For both Tina and Jack, their grief was damaging their relationships – Tina was aware of this and wanted to change it; Jack did not. Newer models have brought different measures of what it means to be 'stuck' in grief, and we look at these in the next section.

Despite the acknowledgement (see, for example, Walter, 1996) that phase, stage and task models were not meant to be interpreted narrowly, followed rigidly or applied beyond their appropriate remit, these models have formed the basis for a 'clinical lore' (Wortman and Silver, 1989) that is now being subjected to serious critique and review, and they do reflect some underlying assumptions about grieving that are now questioned. As is often the case in academic work, the critique is helpful in pushing us towards understandings that take better account of what bereaved people and new research are telling us. So let us look at this critique in more detail.

The 'grief work hypothesis'

Underlying the models outlined so far is what has been dubbed *the grief work hypothesis* (Stroebe, 1992). Stroebe and Stroebe identify the following aspects of the concept of 'grief work':

> *The concept of grief work implies a cognitive process of confronting the reality of loss, of going over events that occurred before and at the time of death, and of focussing on memories and working towards detachment from the deceased.* (Stroebe and Stroebe, 1991, p479)

You can probably identify these elements in Worden's tasks, but these are also present in the other models.

Wortman and Silver (1989) outline a series of assumptions that underlie all these conventional understandings of bereavement. They are:

- There is an inevitable period of distress or depression.

- This is necessary; to avoid it is indicative of pathology.

- It is necessary to 'work through' the loss.

- Recovery can then be expected.

Both Stroebe and Schut, and Wortman and Silver, go on to question these assumptions and we will consider shortly the basis of their critique as well as an alternative model put forward by Stroebe and Schut (1999). But first, you might like to compare this with your own experience.

ACTIVITY **3.3**

Reflect upon a bereavement you have experienced and write brief notes in answer to the following questions:

1. Does the 'grief work' hypothesis correspond to your own experience of grief?

2. If so, in what ways? If not, what are the discrepancies?

3. Going on to think more broadly, can you suggest ways in which these assumptions might be unsatisfactory?

Comment

Many people find that the 'grief work' hypothesis does correspond roughly to their experience, and it is perhaps this that has made it seem attractive as a hypothesis. On the other hand, you may have noted that it was true of one bereavement but not of another; that following one death you had no opportunity to experience the distress in a full way because you had to 'keep going'. Perhaps the emptiness that was all that could be identified of this period eventually passed without an apparent 'working through'. Alternatively, you may have had no opportunity to express the loss and see this as indeed a reason why you have not properly 'got over it'. In relation to the third question above, some clues have already been given above about the limitations of this formulation.

- Firstly, it has been found to be too rigid.

- Secondly, these assumptions make no allowance for differences of gender or ethnicity – does everyone grieve in the same way? After all, even if we restrict the debate to bereavement following death, death has very different meanings depending upon the presence or absence of an active religious faith, for example.

- Thirdly, what is 'recovery' meant to consist of? Many bereaved people do not see it as desirable to return to their previous state. You may recall that Worden changed his last 'task' in response to such views (see page 61).

I wonder if other additional issues have arisen from your own experience. We will look now at the evidence from research, which has led to alternative models of grieving.

The research critique

Gender

Differences in the ways in which men and women grieve have been noted by a number of authors (Lister, 1991; Stroebe, 1998; Riches and Dawson, 2000). Typically, research has shown a tendency for men to be more practical in their responses to loss, focusing upon what needs to be done, and on moving on. In contrast, many women focus upon the grief itself and want to express this. In their research concerning the responses of bereaved parents following a child's death, Riches and Dawson (2000) found that such differences could lead to misunderstandings and a lack of mutual support, with partners seeing each other as either 'unfeeling' or 'wallowing in it'. In some instances where the differences were recognised and accepted as valid, they were not a source of conflict but of mutual support – almost an emotional 'division of labour'.

Culture
In relation to culture, a number of authors have documented different ways in which grief may be expressed. In the previous chapter I referred to Wikan's comparison of grieving in Bali and in Egypt (Wikan, 1988). Rosenblatt summarises these findings as follows:

> *It now seems that realities differ so greatly from one culture to another that it is misleading and egocentric to assume that Western concepts apply generally.*
> (Rosenblatt, 1993, p13)

We need to bear this comment in mind in relation to newer models as well as older ones.

Race
Guneratnam (1997) is one of a number of authors who points out that racist practice can be the result of such assumptions of homogeneity. White practitioners may make assumptions about the 'normal' or healthy response that are based upon research findings that have investigated culturally specific responses in a way that is not acknowledged. If they apply these uncritically when working with black service users, responses that are not abnormal may be seen as such. Multi-cultural awareness is only one aspect of anti-racist practice – and can even be counter productive if this is seen as 'dealing with the issue'. Too often the models that we use are seen as 'truth' and generalised inappropriately to other populations.

General applicability
The applicability of these models of grief to other types of loss has been assumed or argued by many authors (for example Parkes, 1996, as already cited). This is not demonstrated in all instances, however (Payne et al., 1999, p2) and can even be undesirable. In relation to disability, for example, we saw in the last chapter that there is criticism of the application of a loss model to the circumstances of those with an impairment (Oliver, 1996; Sapey, 2002). What is lost? From whose perspective? In terms of the social model of disability, the use of a loss model is inappropriate, since it is society's responses to those with an impairment that create disability. Keith (1994) has put together a powerful collection of writings by women with disabilities, in which this issue is debated. The general question of the applicability of these models to other circumstances of loss is one that will be considered further in Chapter 4.

The views of bereaved people
Ironside (1996) brings together a number of comments from bereaved people who find the concept of 'moving on' to be problematic from a lay perspective, whilst the edited collection of papers by Klass and associates (1996) gives a more academic, research-based view along the same lines. Of course, all research is based upon the views of people who are themselves affected, and the research of Kübler-Ross, Parkes and Worden is no exception to this. This is why it is important that we are specific about the research underpinning theoretical frameworks, acknowledging too that things change over time and that findings can become outdated.

We can conclude then that these models have serious flaws when applied uncritically. As we have seen, part of their appeal is the way in which they do echo our own experience in many ways. And, of course, many (or even most?) practitioners do not use such frameworks in a rigid way, but adapt them and are hopefully guided by the service user they are working with (Lloyd, 2002). Nonetheless, we need to look now at other ways of understanding grief.

Alternative models

In the past ten or twenty years, alternative models have been suggested which meet some of these criticisms, and these have been found useful by practitioners. We will look at three before considering the theoretical roots that underpin these and the earlier models described in this chapter. The first draws upon a tradition of psychological studies of reactions to pressure and stress, and the others focus upon the social process of reconstructing a person's internal world following the profound disruption brought about by loss.

The 'Dual Process' model of coping with bereavement

In a paper first presented at a conference in 1995, Stroebe and Schut have put forward a model of coping with bereavement that suggests that people have to cope with two stressful aspects of their situation following bereavement. This in turn leads to two orientations following bereavement:

- 'loss orientation', encompassing all that was previously described as 'grief work', such as remembering the lost person and focusing upon what is no more;

- 'restoration orientation', in which the person is addressing the changed demands that arise from the loss, such as coping with its aftermath, doing new things and being distracted from grief.

The authors argue that both orientations are an essential part of grieving, and are necessary, but most important of all is that there should be movement, or *oscillation*, between them. Pathological grief arises when there is no such movement – for example, when someone can only focus upon new things and refuses to remember and to grieve, or (conversely) when they will not attend to the future or to practical matters. An important feature of this model is the recognition that socialisation (into both cultural norms and gender roles) affects the balance between these orientations. Thus, the tendency for men in European societies is often to focus upon restoration (Stroebe, 1998; Riches and Dawson, 2000), whilst for women it is more socially acceptable to focus upon grief. Similarly, in relation to culture, Stroebe and Schut (1998) suggest that this may explain the different responses in Egypt and Bali described by Wikan (1988), which were referred to in the previous chapter.

This 'dual process model' has gained in credibility amongst both academics and practitioners since it seems to overcome many of the criticisms already outlined, whilst retaining some of the important aspects of earlier models.

Think of a bereavement situation known to you. This could be from your own experience, from the experience of a friend or service user known to you, or from the media (newspapers or TV or film).

1. *List aspects of the response of the person affected that seem to you to arise from a loss orientation, and those that seem to reflect a restoration orientation.*

2. *Based either on the brief outline here, or preferably upon reading Stroebe and Schut's own account of the model (1998 or 1999), consider the strengths and weaknesses of this model in the light of this practical example. Make a note of your thoughts and rationale.*

Comment

In relation to the loss orientation, you probably noted features such as talking about the dead person, crying, visiting the grave. In relation to restoration orientation, you may have mentioned selling the house, or looking for a part-time job, or taking up a new hobby.

I wonder what your response was to the second question. Most people seem to find more strengths than weaknesses, and that Stroebe and Schut's model makes sense and is a useful therapeutic tool. You will find a discussion of its application in social care situations in Currer (2001), as well as some worked examples. One of the aspects that has come up in class discussions of this model is the observation that the ability to engage in restoration-orientated activities may be limited by discrimination. One student gave the example of a man with mild learning difficulties who sought to enrol on a course, but was discouraged by the reactions of others: this experience reinforced his loss rather than offering an opportunity for restoration or distraction from grief. There are links here with Doka's (1989) work on disenfranchised grief, already introduced in Chapter 1. If we compare this model with Worden's tasks, we can see that the first two tasks are more concerned with 'loss orientation' and the last two with 'restoration orientation'. It is an explicit aspect of Stroebe and Schut's model, however, that there is ongoing movement between these orientations, rather than a neat progression, although they do suggest that loss orientation may be more predominant early on.

CASE STUDY

Sally had two young children and when her husband left her, she put their needs first and concentrated on sorting out their new house and getting them resettled in new schools. Friends commented that she seemed to be managing very well. It was not until the death of the family rabbit the following year that she became very distressed and realised that she had not made an opportunity to grieve.

We might see Sally as being forced into restoration mode. In contrast, another person might find that they are stuck in looking backwards and focusing on their grief.

Margaret Stroebe is a Professor of Psychology who has conducted research into bereavement. It is not surprising therefore to find that model drawing upon this background. The models considered next derive from sociological work on identity and the ways in which identity is understood and constructed.

Tony Walter's 'New Model of Grief'

Walter (1996) has pulled together many of the criticisms of earlier theories that we have already looked at, and is particularly interested in the idea of 'moving on' after a bereavement, and in how this is accomplished. The death of his father and of a close friend gave him the impetus to explore these matters, and he proposes that the purpose of grief is not to move on, but to sustain a bond with the person who has gone. Clearly that bond must now be of a different nature. He suggests that the purpose of grief is not detachment, but resolution by *finding an appropriate place* in our lives for the relationship that is now so altered. For Walter, the funeral can be a significant event in this process, which is essentially a social one and conducted with others by talking about the dead person. He points out that many people want to do just this, but that in modern society it can be difficult because our lives are often so fragmented. He highlights evidence from bereaved people who find that conventional models of bereavement make no sense for them, as we have already discussed. As we shall see when we look at underlying theories, this model is in line with sociological and social psychological ideas about the construction of self – the funeral is part of this process of creating the identity of the bereaved person – writing the final chapter, if you like.

Walter's emphasis (it does not really amount to a 'model' in the same ways as others) came partly through the experience of planning a funeral for a very close friend. Have you ever had to do this? The next activity asks you to write your own obituary. This can be a good way of trying to identify your hopes and aspirations, and of illustrating the way in which our 'self' is socially constructed. This can be distressing, however, so do not feel that this part of the activity is essential. If you like, you can omit it, or else make sure that you have an opportunity to 'debrief' with a friend afterwards.

ACTIVITY 3.5

Write your own obituary. What does this tell you about the 'self' you aspire to be?

In your view, what is the purpose of a funeral for those who are left?

Do you agree with Walter that the purpose of grief is not detachment, but a 'relocation' of the deceased? What does this idea mean for you?

Comment

One's own view of oneself (as reflected in the obituary that you have drafted) may of course be very different from what others will say about you. For Walter, the funeral is important precisely because the images and memories that we have of someone we have cared about are very different to those of others. Part of the purpose of the funeral is to fit this 'jigsaw' together. For some people, Walter's paper describes their own feelings exactly. One student spoke of her friend whose daughter had died tragically. For the mother, the opportunity to meet her daughter's friends and to listen to their tributes to her, were very significant. This helped her to understand her daughter's life more fully, to find some meaning in what had happened, and to lay her daughter to rest.

For people with a definite religious belief, the idea of 'relocation' may refer to a sense of the person in a 'better place'. For others, this may not be so, and it may mean finding a place in their own life that is especially associated with the person – this could be their grave, a favourite tree or place, or a part of the house. These are all actual places, but the idea is much broader than this, and refers to finding a way of thinking about a person, perhaps talking to them – a way of relating despite the fact that they are physically absent. Klass et al. (1996) found that many young people were in the habit of talking over big decisions with a deceased grandparent, for example.

Meaning Reconstruction Theory

Neimeyer (2000) is interested in the fact that apparently similar crises can have very different outcomes for the individuals involved. Why do some people seem to become stronger after a tragic bereavement whilst others are destroyed by it? The next activity asks you to consider what factors make a difference.

ACTIVITY 3.6

Consider this scenario. Two young children have been killed together in an accident at a playground. They have similar home circumstances, and both have one older and one younger sibling. One mother is destroyed by the accident; the other finds that after some time, this experience has brought deeper meaning to her life. What do you think may be of importance in leading to the different effects here? Make a note of your suggestions.

Comment

I wonder if you mentioned factors such as religion, or the presence of social support? Neimeyer and Anderson (2002) give an example that is very similar to this one – the different responses of two mothers to the death of an infant daughter through congenital heart problems. In their example, the women both had good support and a religious faith, yet their ability to find meaning was totally different, as in our example here. Meaning reconstruction theory rests on the idea that traumatic loss threatens all that we take for granted. It may just as easily threaten a religious faith as confirm it. This may remind you of Marris's observation that loss is like finding the law of gravity to be invalid (see page 54). Anyone affected by a profound loss has to reconstruct all the meaning that was previously taken for granted. This happens in three senses:

- Firstly, we ask 'why', and need to make some sort of sense of the loss itself. This is not just an individual process, nor is it once and for all. Early answers are likely to change, but this doesn't matter; it is being able to find meaning that matters.

- Secondly, we look for benefit in the experience (such as making us a better person or more sympathetic to others). This does not make the loss worthwhile, but it is part of finding meaning.

- Lastly, we must 'relearn the self' – rediscover who we are, now that one special relationship has been disrupted. Since the self is social, we who are left are no longer the same.

This process is one that unfolds and develops over time. Although professionals can help, they must follow the process, not direct it. Neimeyer and Anderson's description draws upon studies in which we can see people benefiting greatly from 'telling the story'. It is not the empathetic manner or skill of a therapist or listener that makes the difference here; benefits have been found when people speak into a tape recorder, or write their tale, and then destroy what has been written. Pennebaker (1997) invited bereaved people to write for 20 minutes a day over three or four days, and positive benefits were demonstrated using standardised measures of wellbeing, even when the scripts were destroyed by prior agreement. Most people, Neimeyer and Anderson argue, find the search for meaning in loss to be 'compelling'. They say that *bereavement is, amongst other things, a crisis in meaning* (2002, p62).

Common themes

In all the theoretical models that we have considered, there seem to be some common themes. You may recall that in Kübler-Ross's phase of anger, there was a search for meaning – 'Why me?', people ask when faced with a terminal diagnosis, 'Why now?' One of Colin Murray Parkes's early contributions were to point to loss as involving a 'psycho-social transition' or revision of all that had been taken for granted.

In this chapter, we have looked at a large number of different ways in which grief and bereavement have been understood. Walter (1997) has described recent changes in the popularity of received wisdom and of accepted models as a 'revolution' in thinking in this area. Yet the two themes of coherence and control, which were introduced in Chapter 1, can be seen to run through both old and new models. These two themes were identified by Antonovsky in his (1987) research concerning the meaning of health. He asked a very similar question to that posed by Neimeyer and Anderson, although Antonovsky was interested in the responses of Jewish people who had survived the Holocaust: 'How was this possible?' The answer concerned the importance of meaning. For those who could find some meaning in their situation at whatever level, and who were able to establish some control (however small) over an aspect of daily life, survival (meaning in this case survival not only at a physical level but also mentally) was possible.

In relation to grief as well as to health, these two themes are central. We have seen how 'meaning' (which is very close to coherence) has been an element in all the models, from Marris's early work on the 'structures of meaning' to more recent formulations. Control relates to powerlessness. Grief is very closely associated with powerlessness. As we saw in the Chapter 2, it can arise from it. More importantly, however, one of the major feelings associated with grief is the loss of control (Bright, 1996; Ironside, 1996). This again has close links to the 'helplessness and hopelessness' that are characteristic of depression.

Theoretical bases and concepts

Deliberately, I have introduced you to models of grieving before considering the theoretical perspectives that underlie them. This is because the area is one in which practice models and descriptions of peoples' responses have often preceded rather than followed theoretical development. As I have tried to show, practice concerns have frequently been the driving force. Yet we can also identify four main theoretical positions behind these models.

Psychodynamic theory

In 1917, Freud published a paper called *Mourning and melancholia*, in which mourning was seen as a painful process of withdrawing energy from memories of the lost person. His brief outline has been very influential. Hagman (2001) outlines the features of what he calls the *standard psychoanalytic model*. These are:

- that *there is an identifiable, normal, psychological mourning process*;
- that the function of mourning is restorative (back to the status quo), not transformative;
- that this process is internal and psychological, not social;
- that the process is natural and feelings should not be suppressed;
- that there are shared commonalities in the process of normal grieving;
- sadness is most characteristic;
- there is an emphasis on detachment not continuity;
- meanings are not emphasised;
- mourning has an end, it is not ongoing.

Hagman goes on to review changes that more recent writers in the psychoanalytic tradition have made and to propose a new definition and model that incorporate the importance of meaning making. However, we can see from his analysis of the original assumptions how these have influenced a number of approaches to bereavement counseling and models of grieving. Whilst Lindemann's early work specifically sought to delineate the characteristics of normal grieving, and followed Freud's interest in outlining pathological forms, some of the assumptions underpinning later models can also be seen as being aligned to the characteristics outlined above. The current 'revolution' in thinking is questioning a number of these, looking at social rather than only psychological approaches and at continuity of relationships.

Attachment theory

Social workers are familiar with attachment theory which has been very influential within social work generally. As already noted, Bowlby (1971) outlined a number of phases of grief. Parkes (2006) offers a review of the ways in which attachment theory has considerably influenced the understanding of grief and grieving. His own work is rooted in this tradition, as is that of Worden and Bright, amongst others. Attachment theory sees the basis of an individual's grief response not in internal psychic processes, but in patterns of behaviour and response that have been learned very early in life. Later relationships (and losses) are moulded by this early experience and the pattern of attachment that it has created – patterns that have been classified by Ainsworth and other colleagues (see Parkes, 2006, for an overview).

A number of writers have criticised assumptions that attachment theory is universally applicable, suggesting that some of its assumptions are Eurocentric (see Gambe et al., 1992). Although early formulations were used to reinforce post-war policies of keeping women at home (since the attachment figure was originally assumed to be the mother), subsequent work has led to modification and adaptation with ongoing research. More recently, cross cultural work has explored both the limits and broad applicability of the patterns of attachment described (see Robinson [2007] who has considered the various issues and the latest research). Since some of the models of grieving have this as their root, we must ensure that they do not perpetuate assumptions about the universality of responses to loss when attachment theory itself has adapted in the light of more recent work.

Stress, crisis and coping

Whilst pressure is a normal feature of life, stress has been defined as *your response to an inappropriate amount of pressure* (Arroba and James, 1987 p3). Prolonged stress can obviously lead to losses (such as the loss of one's health) or can indeed be caused by a particular loss (such as a relationship breakdown). Many losses result from some sort of crisis, but crises themselves may be sudden and unexpected, or brought about by long-term ongoing pressures. Crisis intervention is a therapeutic approach that has not, to date, been explicitly linked with loss and grieving, but some argue that there is scope for such links to be made (Thompson, 2002a).

Work that has been drawn into theorising about loss and grief is that on stressful life events (Holmes and Rahè, 1967) and on stress and coping (Lazarus and Folkman, 1984). Payne et al. (1999) have usefully reviewed this literature and its contribution to understanding loss and grief. The work on life events tended to see certain events as simply being negative and ignored the meaning that they have for those affected. The literature on coping takes more account of positive and psychological aspects, but is still very individual in its focus. Nonetheless, this body of work has formed a basis for Stroebe and Schut's 'Dual Process Model' (1999). It also underpins some of the work on resilience which will be considered in the next chapter.

Narrative approaches

Within sociological theories concerning the social construction of identity (Giddens, 1991), the 'self' in postmodern society is continually negotiated and recreated in the processes of social interaction. In other words, we build up a view of ourselves through the responses that others make to us, and we also manipulate this response by aiming for a certain 'self'. This sounds complicated but is actually very familiar – you only need to watch any teenager in their bathroom to see the construction of a 'self', and we are familiar with the concept of an 'image' created deliberately by spin doctors for politicians or media stars. Symbolic interactionism – the forerunner of the constructivist approach – would see this as an artificial example of an ongoing natural process in which we are all constantly involved. Our lives are like a story or novel, which is why these approaches are called 'narrative approaches'. When loss threatens the 'storyline', we have to work at revising it in line with the new reality.

Narrative approaches have both sociological and psychological aspects. They can be applied on a grand scale to the biographies of groups or societies (for example, many of the colonial 'histories' have been criticised as being only one side of a story), or at an individual level to see how people make sense of their own changed world following trauma or bereavement. Both Walter's model and Neimeyer's work fall within this social constructivist approach.

Conclusion: Overall themes and strands

Social work has its roots in both psychology and sociology, and we can see that until relatively recently, theories and models of grieving have drawn more heavily on psychological and individual explanations and theories. Yet this balance is now being redressed, and it can be argued that this restoration of the social dimension within the theory base in relation to loss and grief has particular importance for social workers. There is also considerable overlap. In attempting to make distinctions in order to clarify the issues at stake, it is important that we do not set up a false polarisation.

Integration?

Despite the different theoretical starting points of these approaches to understanding grief, there are remarkable similarities between them. In their most recent book, Kübler-Ross and Kessler (2005) repeat the assertion that the stages were never meant to be rigidly applied, and suggest also that the situations of adjusting either to a terminal diagnosis or following a bereavement are all about meaning. In his (2006) book, Parkes comments on the Dual Process Model and sees this as integrating attachment theory and his earlier work on assumptive worlds. Walter (1997) identifies the strands of newer arguments in older viewpoints, suggesting that this is a case of minor and major themes within different models – a matter of emphasis. Both he and Stroebe and Schut have discussed the relative merits of their different emphases in a published exchange (see Stroebe, 1997; Walter, 1997). Stroebe and Schut have in turn contributed to Neimeyer's (2002) volume on meaning reconstruction, and have agreed about the centrality of meaning making in the process of adjustment following bereavement.

It seems, therefore, that differences – at least between the more recent formulations – are differences of emphasis only, despite their varying philosophical and disciplinary underpinnings. As the title of Water's reply to Stroebe suggests, it is the tension between 'letting go' and 'keeping hold' that is at the heart of the debate – the very tension that Stroebe and Schut's model itself highlights. Rightly or wrongly, earlier formulations emphasised the former, and this emphasis is now rejected in favour of approaches that prioritise the integration of past experience. No doubt the different underpinning theoretical approaches will drive research in new and different ways, but for now the recent 'revolution' in thinking around models of grieving seems to have reached a more even keel.

What is important for the practitioner to know?

In the face of such theoretical debate, you might well ask what it is that a practitioner needs to know. In the next chapter, we will consider this in more detail, looking at the extent to which these models have been used in relation to different areas of loss and at some of the problems with the rigid application of any theoretical model. We will end with a suggested framework for practice. To round off the current discussion, however, the following points are worth making.

- The experience of grief is unique, but there do appear to be some common elements.

- Awareness of these commonalities can be reassuring for some people, since one of the aspects of grieving is that it is often a new and frightening experience – some landmarks can therefore be useful, as long as they are not used proscriptively.

- The experience is one which involves body, mind, heart and spirit, although the balance between these aspects is different for everyone.

- At the heart of the process of grieving there is a tension between letting go of the past and keeping hold of it in a way that is meaningful.

We have been speaking as if grief were only one thing, whatever its cause, despite having tried to be aware of the dangers of this. In the next chapter, we look critically at the applicability of the models outlined so far to areas of loss other than death, extending the discussion that has been started in this chapter. Given that meaning making is seen as central in the process of grieving, it would indeed be surprising if the different ways in which events such as death may be understood were not a factor in the response to loss.

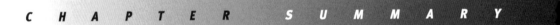

C H A P T E R S U M M A R Y

This chapter has introduced and discussed a number of different theories and models of grieving. Its intention has been to offer you an overview of work to date, and I hope that you now have a broad understanding both of earlier approaches and the more recent ones in which some of the implicit assumptions have been challenged. You may also, through the various activities, have your own view of the importance of the various strands that have been identified here. The next chapter will offer an opportunity to develop this further.

FURTHER READING

Walter, T (1996) A new model of grief: bereavement and biography. *Mortality*, 1 (1): 7–25.

This is the paper in which Walter originally outlined his 'new model'.

Stroebe, M and Schut, H (1999) The dual process model of coping with bereavement: rationale and description. *Death Studies*, 23 (3): 197–224.

This is the paper which outlines the Dual Process Model of grieving. Look in the references at the end of this book for other papers by the same authors relating specifically to the role of culture and of gender.

Neimeyer, R and Anderson, A (2002) Meaning reconstruction theory. In Thompson, N (ed), *Loss and grief*. Basingstoke: Palgrave.

This chapter is probably the most accessible introduction to meaning reconstruction theory, although you might wish to look at other papers by Neimeyer as well.

Goldsworthy, K Kellie (2005) Grief and loss in social work practice: all changes involve loss, just as all losses require change. *Australian Social Work*, 58 (2):167–78.

A useful review of the theory base and its relevance for social work, and a powerful argument for teaching about loss in social work training.

Chapter 4
Linking theory and practice

Introduction

The last chapter introduced you to a number of models of grieving. In this chapter, we ask how useful these are likely to be for you as a practitioner. Although the use of case studies has sought to illustrate the relevance of all that has been covered, that is not the same as focusing on the question of the applicability of understandings of loss and grief in social work practice. To a certain extent, this is a question that only you can answer – which is something you will be asked to do via a number of activities. To help with this, I will offer a framework that has been suggested as a means to this end – the 'determinants of grief'. These are simply a series of questions, which have emerged as significant from research into bereavement, that can guide your understanding of any loss. We will also review some of the evidence so far, and remind ourselves of some of the question marks that have been raised about the use of a 'loss' perspective. I will consider in more detail the concept of 'ambiguous grief' (Boss, 1999) – mentioned in Chapter 1 – and its associated theory and practice applications. After that, I will discuss the concept of resilience – why is it that some people seem less badly affected than others (both in terms of their physical health and their psychological wellbeing) in the face of loss and grief? We will conclude by looking at ways in which theory can guide practice, but also at ways in which it can be abused. But first, I want to consider loss and grief in childhood and in old age – the two ends of the life span.

Loss and age

In this section, we will consider loss and grief at the beginning and end of the life span, concentrating especially on aspects of loss that are distinctive. It is important to remember that many aspects of the response to loss and grief are unaffected by age in any direct way. I mentioned in Chapter 1 that age can be one of the bases upon which grief may be 'disenfranchised'. Assumptions may be glibly made that children don't feel grief as deeply as adults, or that in old age the frequency of experiences of grief and loss renders them somehow less distressing (Thompson, S, 2002). Writing of loss in relation to older people, Sue Thompson comments:

> One of the effects of ageist ideology is to hide the nuances of individual experiences under 'blanket' assumptions, and to neglect the meaning that individual people attach to specific loss experiences. (2002, p166)

Such is not my intention here. Yet there are certain things that can be said about losses in childhood and in later life that can alert practitioners to aspects of experience that are common by reason of age, and which may therefore be important to keep in mind in work with individuals.

A child's loss

A consideration of losses in childhood is of particular importance for social workers. You may be working in children's services, but even if this is not your situation, these losses have far-reaching effects. One childhood bereavement project known as 'Winston's Wish' (whose services include a residential weekend camp) was set up by two professionals from the field of adult mental health who were struck by how many adults on their caseload had had experiences of unresolved childhood bereavement. Within specialist multi-professional teams in palliative care, it is often the social workers who have special responsibility for work with children and families (Monroe, 1998). Yet whilst death-related losses have an impact in mainstream services as well as in specialist settings (Currer, 2001), it is the losses of looked-after children that are likely to be uppermost in our mind as we consider the impact of a child's experience of loss within social work practice. Whether or not you are engaged in direct work with children, the losses – of all kinds – that are experienced in childhood are likely to be of significance in your area of practice, so it is important that you appreciate some of the issues.

Do models and theories of loss apply?

As we have seen, one of the sources of the models and theories relating to grief is attachment theory and studies of the experience of young children separated from their primary caregivers. It would be surprising therefore to find that such models are not applicable in the case of a child experiencing loss. Various studies have looked at links between the attachment patterns formed in childhood and a later ability to cope with grief and loss (Parkes, 2006). In addition, the pattern of loss described by Bowlby (1971) has been applied in work with children in a variety of loss situations. Working for the courts and making custody recommendations in situations of divorce, Kroll (1994, 2002) found this to be a useful theory base for her work assessing children. She also refers to the work of Jewett who has written about the responses of children in a number of contexts such as fostering and adoption. Jewett (1984) outlines three phases of grief in children.

- 'Early grief' characterised by shock, numbness, denial, disbelief and alarm;

- 'Acute grief' in which there is yearning and protest, similar to that described by Bowlby, and 'searching';

- Integration, characterised by a sort of resignation that 'the worst has happened and I have survived'.

Mallon (1998, p31) draws on the same theory base, but uses slightly different terminology.

- Phase 1 – Early Grief: the protest phase.

- Phase 2 – Acute Grief: the disorganisation phase.

- Phase 3 – Subsiding Grief: the re-organisation phase.

You will no doubt recognise these aspects of grieving from earlier chapters. For children, as for adults, it is accepted that phases may not be sequential and may recur.

In relation to the third phase of grieving, Mallon makes the point that here there is a *conflict between the need to 'let go' in an emotional sense, and the wish to hold on* (1998, p41). Here we have echoes of the oscillation that is key within the Dual Process Model. Stroebe and Schut (1999) see oscillation as occurring throughout the grieving process, not just in a final phase, and although there is as yet less published work on applying this framework in work with children, we can see how it might be applicable. Take the example of Gemma.

Many looked-after children have to make rapid adjustments following serious losses that

Gemma was seven years old when she came abruptly into the care of the local authority following her mother's attempted suicide and subsequent involuntary admittance to the local mental hospital. There had been concerns for some time about Gemma's situation, and the initial emergency short-term care order was later extended. She was placed with foster parents in a town some distance from her home, and started at a new school the following week.

Everything was new for her and she had to adapt very quickly to the challenges of fitting in. Her foster mother was impressed by the way in which she threw herself into the new situation, and quickly made friends. She did not seem to want to talk about her mother, and appeared unresponsive and withdrawn when she saw her, simply asking when she could go back to playing.

Not until some time later did she suddenly break into tears and become angry when she was playing with a friend and making 'daisy chains' – it turned out that this was something that her mother used to do with her when she was much younger.

involve the loss not only of a key person or persons but also of their total environment – pets, school, neighbourhood, daily routines. Gemma appears to have chosen to throw herself into her new situation, and it is hard to say if her response was the result of behaving as she felt she was expected to do or because she had to cope with so many new situations simultaneously. In terms of the Dual Process Model, looked-after children are often forced into 'restoration' mode – with little opportunity to focus upon their loss. In some situations, it will be important for them to be able to retrace their origins, and to go back to 'say goodbye'. If this is not actually possible for practical reasons, the child may be able to do this in a symbolic or ritual way with the help of a sympathetic adult. Jewett (1984) argues that all children in care need the opportunity to say goodbye and also to be given permission by their former carers to be happy in their next placement. This is important and may be difficult – children are well aware that their natural parents often do not wish them to go, and even foster carers may be resentful of a move when a placement breaks down. A child may feel disloyal to a former carer if they are happy after leaving them.

For many looked-after children, loss is the norm rather than the exception. In such situations, we can see the relevance of a particular type of intervention that links with another of the theoretical models that we considered in the last chapter. This is 'life story work' (Rose and Philpot, 2005). A method also used with children in situations where a parent or carer is dying, this has been increasingly recognised as a valuable therapeutic intervention in work with other children who have experienced a series of losses. Through the construction of a 'life story book' which is theirs to keep, a child discovers, talks through and records their own story in the context of a therapeutic relationship. We have already seen the importance of meaning reconstruction for adults. This can be even more important for children for three reasons.

Firstly, the basic facts of what happened and why may simply not be known to a child. Secondly, their ability to understand these facts will change as they grow older – a young child does not have the ability to understand things in the same way as they will when they get older. For this reason, it may be necessary to tell a child about the circumstances of a loss on several occasions as they get older. John's story illustrates this point.

CASE STUDY

John's father committed suicide when John was three years old. His mother told John what had happened in a simple factual way, and made sure that he was included in the funeral. The family then moved house and John's mother met another man and re-married.

Because of the unhappiness around the time of her first husband's death, and her own confused feelings about his suicide, John's mother decided to put the past behind her and was reassured that John appeared to be happy with his stepfather, who was very fond of him. She used to tell her friends that John was really too young to understand. He doesn't seem to remember his father'.

One day John astounded his mother by asking when his father was coming back.

As we shall see below, children do not realise until they reach a certain stage of cognitive development that death is final. John needed to hear this again when he was old enough to appreciate its significance. A life story book can be reread as a child gets older, so that the story can be understood afresh in the context of new experiences and at a later stage of understanding. Apart from the importance of appreciating the influence of cognitive development in early childhood, we all know that certain experiences make different sense with greater maturity – for example, the decision of a mother to give a child up for adoption will be differently perceived by that child when she herself has children. Thirdly, a life story book may provide a child whose experience has included multiple successive losses with a means of constructing identity – a theme that is significant within the understanding of grief as 'meaning reconstruction'.

In looking at the ways in which the various models and theories of grieving may apply in the case of children, I have already referred to some differences of which we need to take account, and so we turn to these next.

What is different about a child's experience?
Broadly speaking, two particular factors need to be taken into account when considering a child's grief. The first is one that I have already mentioned – different levels of understanding that correspond to the different stages of cognitive development. You will perhaps be familiar with Piaget's Stages of Cognitive Development, which depend upon physical maturation, experience, what we learn from other people and a concept called 'equilibration', which means balancing the assimilation of new ideas with changing old ways of seeing things to accommodate new understandings (Beckett, 2002). We can highlight some of the effects of these stages for a child experiencing loss as follows.

- **Infancy (0–18 months)**. It is fear of separation and the emotions of adults that are the important factors at this age, since a child will have no understanding of the actual event. Infants who sense that adults are upset or whose main carer is absent can become distressed and clingy. It is important to keep routines as consistent as possible for a very young child.

- **18 months to seven years**. At this stage, children typically do not understand the permanence of death, but see it as reversible and temporary. Children at this age are ego-centric and see events as caused by or related to themselves; thus death or other disasters may be seen as resulting from their own anger or death wish, or as punishment of their wrong doing. Possible behavioural reactions can include reverting to bed-wetting or baby talk in some cases, although other children may seem unconcerned. Whilst talking may help to make an event real for a child, the blunt questions or remarks of young children can seem inappropriate to adults. Euphemisms can be especially problematic, as they will be taken literally. It is important to be very clear, to avoid such euphemisms, to explain what is happening and to respond to the need for security.

- **Seven to twelve years**. Older school-aged children will gradually begin to appreciate the reality of events such as death, and their irreversibility. There may be a whole range of behavioural reactions, including hostility towards the person who has died, withdrawal and bodily aches and pains. They also need straightforward and honest explanations, and the reassurance that their feelings are acceptable.

- **Adolescence (12 +)**. This is a time of searching for identity. Crises and losses at this time can be particularly difficult, despite the fact that understanding is no longer as limited as it is for younger children. How do you become independent from someone who has already left you? Whilst some may assume a more adult role, others may regress, take risks or become angry and critical. An acknowledgement of feelings is vital, and this can be a time when the involvement of a trusted adult outside the immediate family may be very helpful.

Sam's story illustrates the importance of clarity when communicating with a young child.

CASE STUDY

Sam was four years old when his friend Tim from playschool died. He was taken, along with the other children, to the funeral. Their teacher (a religious woman) took some care to explain beforehand that the coffin contained only Tim's body: the Tim they had played with was not 'really there' any more.

It was not until Sam's grandfather died six years later that Sam – visibly upset, but trying to be 'grown up' – asked his father before they went to the funeral when they were going to cut his grandfather's head off. For Sam, aged four, the distinction between body and spirit that his teacher was trying to make was not understandable – in Sam's mind, 'only the body' meant that something else had happened to Tim's head.

In relation to death, euphemisms abound and are particularly unhelpful. Think of such expressions as 'We lost grandma', or the terrors that can be aroused for a child at bedtime by speaking of the dead as 'sleeping'. Mallon (1998) recounts the story of one child who was terrified many years later by the prospect of an injection after seeing their cat 'put to sleep' at the vet's. A child will often not tell us at the time the connection that is in their mind, as we can see in Sam's case.

I said that two factors affect a child's experience of loss and grief. Cognitive development is the first. The second is that a child is usually not in a position of control. Following a loss, adults are likely (except in traumatic situations of mass tragedy) to have a choice about when or where to move, how to change their life or whether to stay the same. Yet such decisions must be made for a child, simply because they cannot live independently. A child's wishes are frequently secondary to other considerations, even in situations where the care is good. This is the case for children at all times – house moves frequently depend upon adult choices or necessities rather than children's preferences, for example. If you think back to your 'time line' (Activity 1.6, see page 21), it is likely that an unwelcome house or school move may have been part of your own childhood. Most adults are cautioned against making dramatic changes following a major loss – yet children are often expected to do just that, and often with little consultation. This may be a fact of life, but it is no reason to neglect giving a child information or involving them to an extent that is possible. And it is certainly important that we recognise the powerlessness that is also a psychological facet of the experience of grief, which is, for children, very real. Not only could they not control the loss itself, there is often little possibility of any choice or control in its aftermath.

What helps a child experiencing loss?
William Worden and colleagues have conducted a large-scale research study of childhood bereavement in the USA. In this study, children who had experienced the death of a parent were compared with others who had not had this experience but were matched in other respects. All the children involved were living initially with two parents. The report of this study (Worden, 1996) shows how life changed for these children, and emphasises the importance of continued routine activities as well as reassurance and the opportunities to remember and to express feelings. Interestingly, the effects of bereavement were sometimes delayed, with distress shown a few years after the event in changed or disruptive behaviours. Amongst others, two crucial factors identified by the study were the functioning of the surviving parent, which included his or her continued ability to parent the child (some parents became incapacitated by their own grief), and support from peers and others outside the family. As we shall see later in the chapter, the two-parent household where a parent is incapacitated by the loss of their partner (whether through death or other reasons) can lead to a child experiencing a 'double loss' – the actual loss of one parent and the withdrawal of the other. The concept of a 'psychological family' – relevant to this discussion – is introduced below in connection with ambiguous loss, which is relevant for all ages.

RESEARCH SUMMARY

The Candle Project, which is based at St Christopher's Hospice, suggests that children and young people facing loss need:

- *information about what has happened and why, and what is likely to happen next;*

- *reassurance that they are not to blame for what has happened and that they will be cared for;*

- *an opportunity to express their feelings and to make choices about their involvement in any rituals (such as the funeral in the case of a death);*

- *adults who share their feelings and allow children to give comfort as well as receive it.*

(St Christopher's Hospice, 1998)

There are a growing number of good books and other resources available to help those working with children and a list is included at the end of this chapter. Some are for children themselves, others for the adults who work with them. Resources such as board games can help children to discuss their thoughts and feelings in a therapeutic context. Examples include 'All About Me' from Barnardo's, for primary school-aged children, or 'The Grief Game', suitable for older children and published by Jessica Kingsley. Other resources, such as memory boxes and albums, provide ways in which children can collect photographs and other reminders of the people and places that they are leaving, thus enabling them to say goodbye and to move on.

Loss in old age

I have already suggested that loss in old age is frequently, as with young children, trivialised or 'disenfranchised' (Doka, 1989, 2002; Thompson, S. 2002). In old age, personal losses may come thick and fast – the death of one's peers and declining physical health being the most obvious. Sources of self-esteem and self-worth are less readily available in a society where old age is not highly valued. Sue Thompson (2002) rightly attributes such a devaluing of loss in old age to ageism. Therapeutic support is frequently seen as inappropriate for the losses that are experienced at this stage of the life cycle, yet the experience of repeated and multiple losses in a younger person would be seen very differently, as compounding the grief that the person feels rather than making it easier to bear or less important.

Applicability of models of grieving

There is nothing to suggest that the various descriptions of grief and of the grieving process are not useful ways of understanding grief in later life. Indeed, some aspects will be of particular significance. For example, one of the so-called 'determinants of grief' (considered below in more detail) directs us to consider a person's past experience of loss. Whilst such past experience can be seen as building up the experience of coping with loss or grief, it also serves as a reservoir of sadness that may be triggered by subsequent losses. A person with much experience of grief may have developed some ways of managing, and might have found positive ways to integrate these past experiences, but we should not assume that this is the case.

The Dual Process Model of grief looks at the need to oscillate between loss and restoration orientations. For someone who is not very active or who has limited ability or opportunity to go out, the pressures towards restoration may be few. This is not to deny that many older people live full and active lives, but it may be harder for some to create opportunities, and the need to depend upon others for transport or for help in other ways is likely to make restoration more difficult.

If we consider loss as a crisis in meaning, we need to ask about the significance of a loss for the person concerned. Negative societal images of old age are reinforced by any decline in ability. A person who is seen by others as socially invisible or even as a 'burden' will experience any further losses as decreasing their value still further. Both of these processes are seen in the case of Margaret.

CASE STUDY

Margaret was an active 84 year old. She nursed her husband at home until his death, with home carers coming in three times a day. A private person, she deeply resented their intrusion. Carers were frequently late and often there was little consistency, meaning that routines were disrupted and preferences had to be explained afresh. Nevertheless, she was glad of the help that enabled Ron to stay at home.

After his death, she was exhausted, and it took a while to recover her physical health. When she did, she felt useless as well as lonely, despite having good friends. Her mobility was poor, and nothing interested her. She felt that she was a burden on her family. This changed when someone asked if she would take on the job of secretary for a local organisation – something she could do from home.

At first she was reluctant, but she had been an efficient administrator in her younger days and had always been interested in this particular charity, which raised funds for people with the same condition that Ron had had. The challenge of the new job gave her a sense that she still had something to offer. She felt that Ron would have been proud of her, and it gave her a way of honouring his memory. Instead of waiting for her children to call, she was now sometimes out at a committee meeting when they phoned.

Caring for Ron had given Margaret meaning in her life, and when he died she lost this as well as his company. The new job gave her a sense of purpose again.

In general, then, models and understandings of grief are applicable for people in old age as much as for other groups. Yet we must be aware of the pressures exerted by an ageist society to ignore or minimise such losses. Not only is Western society ageist, it is also one in which independence is highly valued. One of the greatest losses may therefore be that of independence. Similarly, cognitive ability is highly valued. Thus dementia, which eventually destroys cognition as well as making it impossible to live independently, is much feared.

An awareness of cultural relativity in the ways in which age is understood can help us to identify the collective cultural assumptions from which ageist attitudes derive. Boss (2006) contrasts Western discussion of such aspects as the stress of caring, or the 'caregiving burden', with the way in which this issue is viewed by the Ojibway people, who are Native American. Amongst the Ojibway, caring for an elderly relative with dementia is seen as a privilege and the normal fulfilment of the 'circle of life'; Western ideas are therefore seen as offensive (Boss, 2006, p29). Such comparisons are salutary – but they are no comfort to a relative who is struggling within their own cultural framework to balance feelings of stress and guilt. In practice, your guide is the service user, their carer(s) and their assumptions and experiences. Later in this chapter, we will consider the ways in which theory may be used in helpful and unhelpful ways.

Particular considerations

One concept that has emerged from research into individuals' responses to a terminal diagnosis has particular relevance for social work with older people (Quinn, 1998). This is the concept of 'social death'. In the 1960s, sociologists Glaser and Strauss (1965, 1968) and Sudnow (1967) observed, in hospital settings, that some patients were treated as being 'dead' before their body had stopped functioning. For example, staff might ignore them whilst attending to their physical needs. This can be linked to Goffman's (1969) work, in which he notes that some people (such as servants) are socially invisible. 'Social death' has been defined as follows:

> The defining feature of social death is the cessation of the individual person as
> an active agent in others' lives, (Mulkay and Ernst, 1991, p178)

Conversely, anthropologists have noted that in some societies social life continues beyond biological death, with people who have technically died still being very much part of social life, in contrast to being excluded before physical death. In parts of Indonesia, for example, the dead person may be 'fed' for some weeks after death (Parinding and Achjadi, 1988), and in many cultures, ancestors play a vital part in rituals and ceremonies. This links to the discussion in Chapter 2 of 'continuing bonds' and also to that below of the 'psychological family'.

A recent sociological definition of dying notes three aspects. For Seale (1998), dying is the *severance of the social bond*. He says that:

> Disruption of the social bond occurs as the body fails, self identity becomes harder to
> hold together, and the normal expectations of human relations cannot be fulfilled.
> (1998, p149)

It is useful to distinguish the three aspects in this definition.

- The body, which includes physical aspects such as continence or physical abilities.

- Self-identity, which covers the individual aspects of the 'self': how we think of, and present, ourselves.

- Human relations and the social expectations that attach to them: this covers matters such as remembering birthdays and attending celebrations.

We can see that these aspects do not always coincide. We are all familiar with older people who are 'all there', but whose body may 'let them down'. Equally, some people who are physically sound may deteriorate in terms of the presentation of the self (perhaps neglecting their appearance or cleanliness), or might be unable to keep up socially. In fact, many people who are afraid of increasing dependence begin to put a great deal of energy into 'keeping up appearances'.

Can you see how this connects with the idea of 'social death'? We are used to thinking of death as a single bodily event, but Seale's analysis helps us to recognise other aspects that may be useful for us as practitioners in understanding what is happening for people. This has relevance at all stages of the life cycle – for example, the person drawn into considering suicide may be physically healthy and apparently well supported socially, but unable to maintain a coherent sense of the self. This has particular relevance for work with older people. The next activity invites you to think of some ways in which this may be so.

ACTIVITY 4.1

Look at the definitions of social death and of dying given above and suggest some situations that may arise in practice where the concept of 'social death' may apply.

Social death in relation to social work practice

This concept has been applied to entry into residential care for older people and to some practices that can occur in residential homes, where residents who are close to death may be separated or excluded from the mainstream of activity (Shemmings, 1996). Sweeting and Gilhooly (1997) have looked at social death in relation to care at home of people with advanced dementia. In their research, they distinguish *believing* that a person is socially dead from *behaving* toward them as if this were so. Thus, many relatives reported believing that 'S/he died some time ago' or 'Isn't really there any more', yet continued to speak to their dependent relative as they cared for them, or to ask their opinion even when they knew there would be no real response. Loss of independence and of one's own home, perhaps through entry into residential care, can be seen as 'the beginning of the end' – a form of social death – however well this is managed. Referring to the threefold definition of dying, we can see how important it is to maintain a sense of the self as active and able, even in the face of a body that can let you down in unexpected ways. 'Keeping up appearances' becomes a time-consuming but vital endeavour if one is to fulfil the 'normal expectations of human relations'.

Practice implications

Implications for practice might include thinking differently about the way in which community care assessments are conducted. For an older person in hospital who may be unable to return to their own home, this assessment may be analogous to the diagnosis of a terminal disease. Just as physical diagnosis can confirm the fear that physical death is imminent, so the assessment of living options may also confirm the fear that a form of 'social death' is about to become reality. Thinking of it in this way underlines the importance of taking time to work through feelings as well as to establish practical options. It is ironic that there is pressure for members of the medical profession to develop greater sensitivity in disclosing terminal disease, but also pressure on care managers to assess people's needs for accommodation in a quick and routinised way. This may be one instance where the use of theoretical concepts by social work managers might strengthen resistance to any cost-cutting that involves negating the feelings of service users.

The relation between death and old age is paradoxical. One the one hand, deaths in old age (in numerical terms the majority of deaths) are often 'left out' of academic and practice discussions of 'dying', which – like hospice care – tend to focus upon 'untimely' deaths at a younger age. At the same time, we need to avoid the automatic association between old age and death – either physical or social death. A quotation from Reoch (1997), cited by Thompson and Thompson (1999), illustrates this well and in a way that echoes our earlier discussion of 'social death'. Reoch says that:

> *One of the most hurtful misconceptions about the process of ageing is the assumption that at some point in their lives people inevitably stop growing personally. This attitude has an insidious effect, like a self-fulfilling prophecy. The result is that older people are all too often treated as if they had already stopped living.* (Reoch, 1997, p14*)*

The argument that we should recognise the seriousness of the move from independent life to increasing dependence on others is based upon the belief that such transitions need to be accorded the importance that they warrant, at whatever stage of life they occur. To dismiss such a momentous life change as inevitable or to ignore its emotional impact is to deny that older people are faced with immense adjustment and loss – often at a time when their personal resources are much reduced.

Let us give the last word in this section to something that emerges from the stereotypes of ageing that are found in novels and other literature. On this basis, Hepworth identifies *the dilemma at the heart of ageing – namely the problem of making sense of the experience of time passing and coming to terms with change* (2000, p36).

Applicability of models of grief

Having considered the ways in which models of grieving may apply to losses in childhood and to those in old age, and looked at the particular considerations that apply at both these points of the life cycle, we turn in the next three sections to a more general consideration of the applicability of models of grieving. This section begins with a reminder of the different situations for which these models have already been seen as relevant, and then gives further examples from losses encountered in social work practice. We look at what have been called the 'determinants of grief' and at how these can be used as a simple checklist for a practitioner seeking to understand the experience of loss. Then we will review briefly a situation in which the use of a loss model has been criticised before considering another theoretical distinction – that of 'ambiguous loss'.

Asking the question

It is important that theoretical models are applied appropriately. One of the problems with thinking and talking about loss and grief is that they are very broad concepts, and it is tempting to apply theoretical understandings and models to a very wide range of situations. For example, it is commonplace to observe that divorce, unemployment and moving home are all forms of loss and therefore have similarities. I have already done this in earlier chapters of this book. Yet Payne et al. would argue that:

> ... *the wide application of models which have not yet been convincingly demonstrated in the field for which they were devised – bereavement – is problematic ...* (1999, p2)

The next activity is one in which you will be asked to explore this issue in relation to a particular area of loss of your own choosing – perhaps one that relates to your own area of practice or interest. A number of areas of loss might be suggested as a starting point for this activity, such as:

- loss of work – e.g. unemployment, redundancy;
- loss of place – e.g. entry into residential care, being a refugee, going to prison;
- parental loss of a child – e.g. through care proceedings, adoption, miscarriage;
- loss of a partner or significant other – e.g. the ending of a relationship, the death of a pet;
- bodily loss, impairment or ageing. This area might include a range of different situations, such as puberty or the menopause, amputation or congenital deafness.

This activity is quite complex and may take some time. It involves looking back at the theoretical ideas – such as the stage models or the Dual Process Model – from the last chapter, as well as further reading or research if this is possible for you. I hope that this will not put you off – seeking to apply theories and models to real situations is a good way of becoming familiar with them, and also of spotting their flaws.

ACTIVITY **4.2**

From the general areas of loss listed above, choose one. Some background reading or research in relation to this topic would be helpful – what is known about this area from research or other writings? Then think of a specific example of someone known to you (or from a book or article) who has experienced this sort of loss.

Choose one of the models outlined in Chapter 3, and see how far you think it applies to this situation. For example, if you choose the Dual Process Model, ask what might constitute a 'loss orientation' and what a 'restoration orientation'. If you choose one of the stage models, ask how far these were evident. Note down your responses and thoughts and examine carefully any problems that seem apparent in relation to the situation of loss that you have chosen.

Comment

Whilst there is a lot of literature on these topics, it is often separate from the literature on loss and grief. Inevitably, your response is likely to be somewhat speculative, as you may be trying to recall or guess what a person was experiencing or feeling.

You may have found situations of loss that perfectly mirror those outlined in theoretical papers. As we saw in the last chapter, Howe et al. (1992) gave very powerful illustrations of each of the 'stages of grief' from the stories of birth mothers. These illustrate shock, yearning, anger, guilt and despair and argue that *the example of women who have given up babies for adoption illustrates many of the strong reactions people experience when faced with a significant loss.* (Howe et al., 1992, p58).

You may recall also that Parkes (1996) concluded that the 'psycho-social transition' associated with relocation or with the loss of a limb is similar to that in bereavement, with all the components of grief present. In a different sphere again, writing about children experiencing divorce, Kroll comments:

> *... mourning is a response to all kinds of loss, rather than being solely associated with the death of a loved one ... all these reactions were relevant to children experiencing divorce.* (Kroll, 1994, p46)

On the other hand, there are important differences when a child is known to be alive and with someone else, as compared to the situation where a child has died; when it is a part of one's own body that is lost rather than a person who has died; when a child's parent is still alive but living elsewhere and perhaps with another family. What effect does this have on such ideas as 'finding a place' for the person who has gone, or those of 'relocation'? You may remember from the last chapter that these ideas are important aspects of the more recent theories of grieving.

Another area of loss – living with a relative with dementia – has been termed a 'living bereavement'. Gilliard (1992) uses Kübler-Ross's model to apply to this situation. She identifies some areas of 'fit' but argues that the emotional process never reaches a final 'acceptance', because the person has not died. Her very short article is a good example of this activity – taking a theoretical model and seeing if it 'fits' another loss situation.

If you have considered the area of bodily loss, some other very important issues may have become apparent. Many people with a lifelong impairment argue that considering impairment as a form of loss is not only unhelpful, but reinforces an individual, rather than a social, model of disability (Oliver, 1996). Within the social model of disability, it is society, not the disabled person, which creates disability. This issue was considered in Chapter 2 (see Activity 2.3, page 39). We saw there that the very idea of what is considered a loss is socially defined. Nevertheless, we cannot, at an individual level, ignore or dismiss the losses for parents and siblings that may result from the presence of a child with a severe disability. That these losses are caused in part by society's failure to recognise the different needs of people who have a disability may be theoretically important, but irrelevant in practice for those involved. Mallon illustrates this movingly through the story of a family struggling to access good services for a child who is blind whilst also caring for siblings who experience significant losses in terms of their parents' time and energy (1998, p107). In this case, as in others we have considered, the perspective of each member of the family may differ. And again, the situation is one that is ongoing – those involved must live with an unresolved and irresolvable situation.

Ambiguous loss

We turn now to consider in more detail a distinction introduced in Chapter 1, where we identified that some losses have no 'closure' or finality. Starting from the premise that absence and presence are not absolutes, Boss (1999, 2006) considers situations where there can be no 'moving on' or 'letting go' because the situation of loss is unresolved and ongoing. In such situations, an individual might, within models of grieving that are stage based and emphasise a goal of detachment, be seen to be failing to grieve appropriately. Yet these situations are ones where the reason for a lack of resolution is external and contextual rather than internal. Although we have already seen that others have criticised the assumption – which originated in the work of Freud – that the goal of grieving is detachment, the situations that Boss describes are ones that are distinctive, yet very common. She refers to such catastrophic situations as war or murder, when there may be a missing body or perhaps no certainty of what has happened, and also to situations such as migration, divorce, mental illness and dementia. Her work is underpinned by research, and also offers a model that can help the practitioner.

Boss's theoretical basis lies in family stress theory, and the theoretical concept that underpins the theory of ambiguous loss is that of the 'psychological family'. Boss points out that the group of people we consider to be 'family' is for all of us broader than those who are actually present, and that uncertainty or ambiguity about who is or is not part of our psychological family immobilises us. How does this apply to the situations of loss mentioned? Boss categorises ambiguous loss as being of two kinds, as we can see below.

RESEARCH SUMMARY

Ambiguous loss

- *Physical absence with psychological presence. Examples include:*

  - *missing persons (perhaps through war, kidnap, natural disasters or runaway children);*

  - *those who have left through moving (such as situations of migration, house or job changes, a child leaving home, a family member in care or prison);*

  - *absent members in families following divorce; biological parents; children given for adoption or who died at or before birth.*

- *Physical presence with psychological absence. Examples include:*

  - *those who are mentally absent for reasons that are serious and irreversible, such as brain injury or coma or dementia;*

  - *those who may be temporarily absent by reason of addiction, mental illness, grief or homesickness – this may even include those addicted to things such as computer games or TV.*

  (Adapted from Boss, 2006, p9)

I wonder if you can see how this relates to earlier discussions, including the situation where a child may 'lose' both carers when one dies and the remaining parent is preoccupied with their loss and psychologically absent.

Boss argues that *ambiguous loss is the most stressful kind of loss* (2006, pxvii). This is because of the high value placed in our culture on ideas of solving and fixing things, and on the cognitive need for clarity. Western society does not tolerant ambiguity well. Moreover, there are not likely to be supportive rituals in many cases of ambiguous loss. Boss's therapeutic work comes from her involvement in such war zones as Kosovo and – more recently – through working with families following the 9/11 tragedy in the USA. Interestingly, she comments that

> *Although more study is needed, I suggest that cultural values, religious and spiritual beliefs, and individual personality traits all influence the degree to which people can temper their need for mastery and tolerate ambiguity.* (2006, p28)

This comment is reminiscent of the study conducted by Ablon (1986 [1973]) which was referred to in the last chapter.

Practice relevance

Boss (2006) identifies six therapeutic goals for working with ambiguous loss. These offer a framework or series of headings that may be useful. They are:

- finding meaning;
- tempering mastery;
- reconstructing identity;
- normalising ambivalence;
- revising attachment;
- discovering hope.

In the first, we can see clear links to the work on narrative, but connections also with the importance of ritual. Mastery is the need to be in control and I have already referred to the work of Antonovsky, for whom coherence and control are key features. It is interesting that these features correspond to the first two goals identified by Boss from her own therapeutic work and research. Loss of any kind undermines our sense of control and we have already seen that one of the features of grief is a sense of powerlessness. This is clearly made worse when the situation is unresolved and ongoing. The third goal here reflects the fact that loss frequently represents a challenge to identity – am I still a wife now that my husband has died, or left, for example? Situations where there is no certainty are clearly a greater challenge. Identity can also include questions about where we belong – studies show that identity may be problematic following migration, for example. Ambivalence is a particular difficulty with loss that is ambiguous – Boss argues here for a need to recognise the existence of ambivalence and to learn to live with the tension of it. Revising attachment is a process that may be seen as being similar to the 'relocation' of a relationship – an aspect that we have already encountered in the models outlined in Chapter 3. The attachment itself is not destroyed by loss, even when a loss is clear and final, and neither is it destroyed in ambiguous loss, but in both it must now be re-understood, re-worked.

Since the lost person remains part of the 'psychological family', there is a link to the continuing bonds described by others. Finally, hope must be realistic and recognise the ambiguity. This links back again to meaning making, and will take different forms for each person. I would argue that these goals are relevant in all situations of loss, although issues of ambivalence and control are raised in particularly difficult ways when the loss is ambiguous in Boss's terms.

Boss's work is much concerned with the idea of resilience, which is discussed later in this chapter. Hers is not an alternative 'model' of grief, but a series of pointers that may be helpful for work in different settings where ambiguous loss is a feature. In common with other theorists from different backgrounds, she challenges any simple notion that 'closure' is either desirable or achievable in many situations of loss.

Determinants of grief

Another tool that may be helpful in working with loss and grief is the checklist of so-called 'determinants of grief' (Worden, 1991), originally drawn up, on the basis of research, in relation to bereavement. These can be slightly adapted to form a series of questions that might be asked about any loss, as follows.

- What or who has gone or been lost? This question is deceptively simple, but one event can lead to many losses. For example, a friend may have died. This friend may be one you saw only once a year, or every day. If once a year, this may be because you took holidays together. If so, the death may represent for you the loss of a pattern of shared holidays, perhaps an inability to go away alone. In addition, we must always be careful to be sure whose perspective is being considered. This was highlighted in relation to the issue of disability, and also in the case studies in Chapter 1, when we considered the ways in which a loss may mean different things for different participants. You will also probably note secondary losses.

- What was the manner or the circumstances of the loss – e.g. was it sudden or long drawn out? Although this is not part of the original model, we might add in here the issue of whether the loss is or is not ambiguous, as well as other dimensions of loss (see Chapter 1) such as rarity, choice and whether the loss is one that can be described as 'disenfranchised'.

- Does the person have a history of losses, perhaps similar ones?

- How does the person experiencing loss usually react to change? This may bring in gender or cultural variables. For example, one person may always react initially by becoming busy, another in the opposite way.

- What manner of social support does he or she have? For adults as well as for children, the existence or not of social support is one of the features most closely linked to positive 'outcomes' in bereavement (Parkes, 1996; Worden, 1996).

These might be issues that you could explore together with a service user, or they might offer a way in which you can better understand what may be going on, before then checking this out with them. The next activity asks you to use this framework, preferably with the example that you chose for the last activity, in relation to the same general area of loss.

ACTIVITY 4.3

Seek to understand the situation you have chosen using the determinants of grief as a framework.

For example, if you previously considered a particular situation of parental loss of a child through the child coming into care, you will need to note the meaning of what the parent has lost; the time taken by the process; the fact that this situation may have little resolution and is stigmatised; the presence or absence of previous such losses and of social support.

I will look at each of the determinants in turn, giving examples from different areas of social work practice and of experience. You will no doubt have come up with your own examples in relation to each category, depending upon the area and specific example chosen.

What is lost?

In looking at the determinants of grief, the first question about 'What is lost?' may well have led to quite a long list. Two examples from very different areas of social work can help to illustrate this – the first refers to a booklet written by mothers whose children had been sexually abused, the second looks at the experiences of older people caring for a spouse with dementia.

RESEARCH SUMMARY

We have found there were many losses in learning that our children had been sexually abused. Some of these included:

- *Loss of home and local friends through having to move*

- *Loss of family support*

- *Loss of confidence in own judgement*

- *Loss of self-esteem*

- *Loss of our children's trust*

- *Loss of being able to grieve the loss of the abuser*

- *Loss of a good image of sex*

- *Loss of trust*

- *Loss of the pleasure of past happy memories of our relationship with the abuser.* (Parents against Child Sexual Abuse, 1995)

The next example is from a totally different area of practice: research with older people.

Both of these are situations that would be described as 'ambiguous'.

RESEARCH SUMMARY

In relation to caring for a spouse with dementia, carers mentioned the following:

- *Loss of previous spousal relationship*
- *Loss of conversation*
- *Loss of freedom*
- *Loss of former social life*
- *Loss of time*
- *Loss of space*
- *Loss of self*
- *Loss of other relationships.*

(Upton, 2001, p2)

Gender considerations can be important in understanding what has been lost. In relation to loss of place, Watson and Austerberry (1986) reported their findings about the meaning of homelessness from the viewpoint of women who are homeless, whilst Fordham and Ketteridge (1998) have also reported gender differences in response to disasters, particularly flooding.

Identifying what has been lost, and also identifying its meaning or significance, can themselves both be therapeutic. Sometimes no-one has asked a person what they miss most about the lost person or situation. It may seem obvious or impertinent to do so. Yet if nothing else, this question offers a way in to helping someone to speak of their loss.

The circumstances of loss

The manner or circumstances of a loss can be very important. In some areas, you will have found many contrasts and may have wanted to explore, for example, the difference between:

- retirement (an anticipated, timely loss of work);
- redundancy, which can be sudden and happen at any age.

Bodily loss is another area offering contrasts between:

- the menopause (gradual expected change);
- amputation (sudden traumatic loss);
- lifelong impairment, (which is maybe not rightly considered a loss at all, as already discussed).

I have suggested that this might also be a place to consider whether the loss is one that is finite or ambiguous, and in what sense; whether it was chosen and whether it is one that is taboo.

History of loss

I remember vividly attending the funeral of a teenaged boy who had died as the result of an accident on his bike. A year before, his elder brother had also been killed in a car crash. For his parents, this was the second death in very similar circumstances. For many service users, losses are a repeat of a similar recent loss – second child taken into care, or a fourth experience of being 'sectioned' under the Mental Health Act, for example. The significance of repeated losses needs to be explored with each individual. We should always beware of assumptions that loss is 'easier' because it has been experienced before. Multiple or serial losses can leave us unable to really absorb or deal with subsequent loss. Many child care workers will be aware of how some children seem 'not to care', yet also of how insecure they are left as a result of repeated losses. The other effect of a history of loss is that patterns of response are developed. Whilst some may be helpful and will contribute to resilience, others may not offer a stable basis for the future, and can become hard to challenge or break through.

Characteristic reactions to loss or change

In Activity 1.2, in Chapter 1 (see page 15), you were asked to look at your own characteristic response to change. In relation to serious losses, personality variables can be important. For example, one person may characteristically become angry, but 'cool down' after a while; another may become very quiet or withdrawn. I know that I always react to bad news by becoming intensely 'efficient', and that it is not until this phase passes that I begin to comprehend or absorb what has happened at an emotional level.

Again, cultural variables influence our characteristic reactions, as we saw in Chapter 2. Gender too is a consideration. Stroebe and Schut (1998, and Stroebe, 1998) have noted the ways in which these impact upon grieving, and you will remember that their Dual Process Model (Stroebe and Schut, 1999) is specifically designed as a model of the grieving process that allows room for such variations.

Social support

It is not surprising that social support should be a factor that affects grieving. In a classic study, Brown and Harris (1978) found lack of support to be one of a number of 'vulnerability' factors in relation to depression. This also emerged as significant in relation to bereavement in Ablon's (1986 [1973]) study of the reactions of Samoan people following a fire, as described in the last chapter. Bereaved people refer to this factor in their own accounts (Currer, 2001, Chapter 7). Stroebe et al. (1996) report on one study that looked more deeply at the precise role of support from family and friends after the death of a partner. They find that social support cannot compensate for the emotional loss resulting from the loss of a primary attachment figure, although it does reduce the effects of social loneliness.

Many of the studies reported so far have considered grieving in terms of individual responses and reactions. We are reminded by family systems theory, however, that there is a dynamic and reciprocal relationship between the responses of all involved. Sutcliffe et al., (1998) are a useful source in relation to this perspective.

Resilience

Increasingly, social workers have become interested in using the idea of 'resilience', which is attractive because of its link with a strengths perspective. Rather than focusing on the negative experience (such as a loss), we want to look at how people survive and even grow through negative experiences. Research can look at what makes this difference – an important question, because if we can answer this, then resources can be targeted towards interventions that ameliorate the effects of loss and trauma. As one author suggests *the promise of resilience is to learn from success* (Fraser et al., 1999). In relation to child care services, Newman (2002) offers a review of the evidence about factors that promote resilience in children – illustrating the potential value of this type of work. Resilience is a factor mentioned by the government in their recent guidance (DfES, 2007) for a review of the new Children and Young People's plans. Within the *Every Child Matters* programme, local authorities must demonstrate in their plan how they will *promote prevention by improving the resilience of children and young people to risk factors* (DfES, 2007, p12). So what is resilience, and how does it relate to our consideration of loss?

Defining resilience

> The term 'resilience' is reserved for unpredicted or markedly successful adaptation to negative life events, trauma, stress and other forms of risk. (Fraser et al., 1999, p131)

Since loss is usually seen both as a trauma and a negative life event, this seems relevant to our topic. But what constitutes a *successful adaptation*?

ACTIVITY 4.4

Think of three loss situations you have observed. These can be from your own experience or in practice settings – it would be helpful to include at least one from each if possible.

What would those most closely involved call 'successful adaptation' in these situations? It may be that this was not achieved but only hoped for.

Comment

In researching the concept of resilience, the way in which 'success' is defined is important but controversial (Fraser et al., 1999). You may have identified that people hoped to regain previous levels of ability and engagement with life that existed before their loss; you may have observed that they hoped to grow stronger as a result. Do we compare what happens afterwards with other people who have not experienced a similar loss, or with others who have (this would give a measure of what might be expected in the particular circumstances), or with the person's own experience beforehand (which may not have included very successful coping anyway)? You will see that in the following definition, the level of functioning is compared with that of the same individual before the crisis:

> Resilience is defined as the ability to bounce back to a level of functioning equal to or greater than before the crisis. (Boss, 2006, p48)

I hope that thinking about this will have alerted you to the fact that this is not a straight-forward issue, and that there is no right answer. Research studies need to specify how they define success, but even then, the use of different definitions makes comparison of studies difficult. This echoes theoretical and definitional issues raised in earlier chapters. Is loss something that we recover from, hoping to return to the status quo, or an experience that may be a source of growth?

Theoretical basis

The idea of resilience has its roots in work on stress and coping, briefly discussed in the last chapter. Early models (such as that of Holmes and Rahé, 1967) classified life events as more or less stressful – the death of a spouse attracted the highest score. Positive events, such as marriage, were also included, which is something that is worth noting since it reinforces the view given in Chapter 1 that loss can accompany change that is both chosen and 'for the better'. Models such as that of Holmes and Rahé were called 'stimulus based models' because they looked at the magnitude of the event, as classified externally. There was no account taken of the meaning for the individual concerned. Lazarus and Folkman (1984) developed a 'response based model' which considered how people respond to stressful events, and two coping styles were identified: *emotion focussed coping; and problem focussed coping* (Payne et al., 1999). Factors that were seen to influence positive responses included: the persons' usual coping style; personality factors; resources both in terms of social support and economic resources; the existence of other concurrent life stressors. These factors are very similar to the determinants of grief that we have just looked at.

Later research on resilience has shown that the individual's belief that they can make a difference is important for how they cope. Ideas of autonomy and the ability to control life, along with the meaning that people ascribe to events, are factors that emerge as being significant. As we can see, these are the very factors that have been identified in more recent theories of grief and loss. Antonovsky's (1987) identification of the importance of coherence and control (see Chapter 1) forms part of the more sociological research base that has contributed to understanding the factors that enhance coping and positive out-comes. We must be cautious, however, in relation to the issue of control and mastery, since these factors may be culturally specific. In some cultures, control and mastery are less important than conformity and being seen to be appropriately fulfilling given roles and social obligations. We know that the ways in which people understand health are culturally variable and also show differences in relation to class and gender (Currer and Stacey, 1986). Although studies of resilience have been undertaken across different cultural groups, the model tends to have an individualistic basis (Payne et al., 1999) and often takes little account of cultural difference. Some see resilience as a personal trait, others as an interactive process. Whilst some authors explicitly include sociological perspectives and see community as a source of resilience, as well as individual factors, others do not. An example of a broader definition is that of Hooyman and Kramer (2006) in their book *Living with loss*, which was written for social workers. They define resilience as:

> *... the behavioural patterns, functional competence and cultural capacities that individuals, families and communities use under adverse circumstances (in this case, loss) and the ability to make adversity (e.g. loss) into a catalyst for growth and development.'* (2006, p66)

They go on to state that finding meaning leads to healthier physical and mental wellbeing.

Overall, the resilience framework is attractive for social workers, but the research evidence is difficult to compare and summarise (Fraser et al., 1999). Although certain factors have been identified as promoting resilience, we need to be cautious about generalisations. In thinking about loss, we are considering a vast number of very different situations, affecting people of different ages, cultural backgrounds and gender. Research findings on resilience are most valuable when they are specific and limited – such as Newman's (2002) review of evidence in relation to looked-after children. For example, this body of research suggests that the presence of a reliable adult outside the family may promote resilience. This factor also emerged from Worden's longitudinal (1996) study of children who had been bereaved, and is a specific finding that has the potential to form a basis for practice. However, the factors that emerge as promoting resilience overall – such as belief systems, social support, and communication skills (Boss, 2006) – look very much like the frameworks we have already considered. Indeed, the determinants of grief which we have looked at in this chapter arose from research into factors (both positive and negative) that influenced outcomes following bereavement. Parkes (2006, p27f, Stroebe et al. (2001) and Payne et al. (1999) are useful sources in relation to this literature.

The identification of risk and vulnerability factors (and hence also of protective factors that enhance resilience) has been used in practice as a means of prioritising resources, but can be very mechanistic and static. Rather than seeing resilience as a characteristic of the person, we should perhaps view it in a more dynamic way. The theoretical models we have looked at suggest that the person who experiences a major loss is thrust into a process of meaning making, in which there is emotional and possibly behavioural disturbance with oscillation between loss and restoration orientations; between looking back and looking forward. This is a turbulent, distressing experience for anyone, and the person needs to be 'held' whilst they are in this process. Couldrick (1995) uses the term *cradling* (following Keenan, 1994) to describe the work of a professional who 'holds' a bereaved family in the period following the death of a parent. We can perhaps widen this concept to include the naturally occurring factors that may be supportive – such as, perhaps, a knowledge of previous losses survived, strong social support, a powerful belief system, or a system of rituals. The image of grieving as a dynamic (albeit painful) process in which a person needs to be supported offers the practitioner a way to assess both if there is a movement in grief (remember that the Dual Process Model suggests that oscillation is a positive sign) and also to look at whether this process is already undergirded or framed in some way, promoting resilience, or whether additional support can be put in place if this is lacking.

The use and abuse of theory

At this point, you may well be rather sceptical of the value of theoretical perspectives. After all, loss is a diverse phenomenon. Pain is very personal. Social work is about listening to the individual. What use are models and theories? I will end this chapter by taking this question seriously and examining the issues more closely.

Are models of grieving helpful?

Consider the following quotes:

> I was crying when they took my Dad away to the Home. The social worker shouted at me 'stop that stupid noise'. I've never forgotten it. (Quoted in Elkington and Harrison, 1996, pp170–1)

> ... social workers tended to see impairment in terms of loss and bereavement. People becoming disabled were believed to go through a grieving process for which the practitioner required special skills ... The consequences of this perspective for practice could mean the setting aside of users' own definitions of their needs and priorities for help'. (Davis and Ellis, 1995, p142)

Although the first situation seems to reflect extremely bad practice whatever the theoretical model, it does also reflect a lack of appreciation of the grief that is involved for both service users and relatives in the momentous life event of entering residential care. The second quote here reflects the use of theory in a way that is inappropriate and also 'blocks out' the service users' own views. Yet theoretical understandings can also be a great help in guiding practice. The next activity asks you to reflect on this in more detail.

ACTIVITY 4.5

Think of a practice situation known to you, and of ways in which loss and grief are features of it. Make a list of the ways in which you think a theoretical understanding or model of the grieving process could be useful for you as a practitioner in that situation (and ultimately therefore for the service users).

Draw up another list of the ways in which this might be harmful. You may have seen colleagues who are either unsure what to do, on the one hand, or over-enthusiastic about a particular theoretical approach, on the other, and this might help you to make these lists.

A form of power: used in whose interests?

Theoretical understandings and professional knowledge are a form of power. Like all power, they can be used positively to further service users' interests and wishes, or as a way of shielding us and promoting our own interests. You might have answered this question at one of two levels.

- At a 'structural level'. By this, I mean that you may have considered ways in which theoretical understandings (or 'professional discourses') can be used generally in society. They can reinforce a mystique of expertise that defines the experience of the service user but does not include him or her. This is an argument that was developed by the French philosopher Michel Foucault.

- In terms of everyday practice situations, fitting people into a favourite theory can lead to not seeing or hearing clients clearly, as we saw in one of the quotes above. Workers can use theory as a barrier to protect themselves, and it can feed assumptions or create labels that lead to oppressive practice. For example, it is possible to dismiss a person's distress or anger on the basis that it is 'expected' in their circumstances. Or we may 'fail to hear' the things that do not fit in with our theories. The ways in which social workers deny loss will be considered in more detail in Chapter 5.

Yet this power can also be used positively in a service user's interests – for example, it can be implemented to argue your client's case at a resource allocation meeting. In the discussion of social death above, I suggested that this concept might be one that strengthens the argument for the need for time to be given to a service user at the point of entry into residential care. Social workers have sometimes acted as if they do not have a theory base to guide their work, which can then be seen by other professionals and managers as being 'wishy washy'.

Conscious frameworks not assumptions
Theoretical ideas can give a framework or starting point, widen our views from our own limited experience, and help us to see a broader rather than a narrower picture. Used flexibly, theories can provide a way of reflecting on our own practice; they can be the basis for analysis – either alone or in discussion with colleagues – and can be used to justify action or to suggest another approach when we seem to be stuck. We need to understand that practice is always guided by some sort of framework – if this is not a body of theoretical ideas, it may be our own prejudices. Whereas theories can be explicitly revised or challenged, unrecognised prejudice is harder to budge.

You may have become rather frustrated with all the perspectives and models outlined in this chapter, thinking that 'it doesn't work like that' in your practice setting. Such a response can be a useful starting point to ask why this is so, and what might be more appropriate. This is how theories and models are developed and changed. To some extent, practitioners have only themselves to blame if their practice experience is not used appropriately to challenge the models that are developed by researchers. Too often, it is a case of the two worlds of theory and practice being separate, with everyone far too busy to engage in debates. The demands of practice are indeed considerable, but we do need to take seriously our responsibility for contributing to the development of practice through models and theories that work for us.

A framework for social work practice

Lloyd (2002) has written about the difficulties that exist with the stage models and theories of grief, and also the way in which social work practitioners find these models at the same time promising and frustrating. In the next chapter, we will consider the use of counselling skills within social work settings, and practitioners' frustration – not just in the UK but across Europe – with what Lloyd refers to as the *post-modern human services context* which no longer values or gives space for approaches such as those outlined here. In her view, social work practitioners do not want a template, but some broad concepts that can offer a more holistic understanding. She argues for a theoretical guide that is broad enough to be applied in diverse, everyday, practice situations. She finds this in the idea of psycho-social transitions, which directs us to what she calls *the loss within* and *the loss without*. She suggests that:

> *... the task of the practitioner is to help the person dealing with loss to reconstruct their inner world so as to re-establish order and consonance with the outer world, where currently they experience chaos and dissonance.* (Lloyd, 2002, pp218–9)

She suggests that this core task links with a number of primary responsibilities, different in each social work setting, such as redefining roles, rebuilding identities, negotiating transition, surviving abuse and maintaining the spirit. This expresses some of the core features of the work of other authors such that they can be used in everyday practice situations. Above all, Lloyd stresses the importance of using any framework flexibly – something that is the essence of reflective practice.

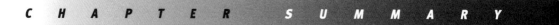

C   H   A   P   T   E   R   S   U   M   M   A   R   Y

This chapter has critically examined the links between theory and practice by looking at the extent to which models and theories of grieving apply to work with children and older people and in social work settings more generally. It has asked you to consider how far the models already described are relevant to your own area of practice or interest and has introduced a checklist that can help you to understand the loss that service users experience in particular situations. These determinants of grief also draw our attention to some of the factors that can influence this experience, and overlap with factors that have been identified as building resilience. Resilience is attractive as a concept that appears to accord with a 'strengths' perspective, but it is most useful when its focus is well defined. Throughout the chapter, we have moved between different situations of loss, in a search to identify both commonalities and areas of difference in respect of situations of loss. The concept of 'ambiguous loss' has been presented as one attempt to make such distinctions in a way that is helpful for the practitioner. Whilst theoretical models can be abused, they give the self-aware and reflective practitioner a starting point and a guide that are more transparent and reliable that the alternative reliance on personal experience or prejudice.

Resources for work with children

A number of organisations now produce a range of products that can be used in work with children in situations of separation and loss. These include:

- a memory store – a coloured box with different compartments in which to keep mementoes;
- a memory book – a system for recording and building up a file of vital information;
- board games that can be used to encourage the sharing of information, hopes and fears;
- books suitable for children of all ages.

These are available from the charities Barnardo's (**www.barnardo's.og.uk/resources.htm**), or Winston's Wish (**www.winstonswish.org.uk/shop**). The latter focuses on death rather than other losses, whilst Barnardo's have many resources for and about work with looked-after children.

Organisations specialising in child bereavement include:

Child Bereavement Project (**www.seelb.org.uk/traumaticgrief/downloads.htm**) which has a list of resources;

The Candle Project (**www.stchristophers.org.uk.htm**) which is part of St Christopher's Hospice and offers resources, events, support and consultancy as well as local services;

Winston's Wish Family Line (**www.winstonswish.org.uk**) which offers support, guidance, advice for families of bereaved children as well as a broad range of resources.

The death of a child (of any age) is a different issue, but it is worth noting the existence of The Child Death Helpline (Freephone 0800 282986, and staffed weekday mornings and every evening 7–10 p.m.). See **www.childdeathhelpline.org.uk** for up-to-date details.

FURTHER READING

Mallon, B (1998) *Helping children to manage loss*. London: Jessica Kingsley

This book takes a broad approach to the different types of loss that children experience, offering suggestions for direct work as well as a good overview of the issues for practitioners. Plenty of case illustrations make this an accessible book.

Rose, R and Philpot, T (2005) *The child's own story – life story work with traumatised children*. London: Jessica Kingsley.

Introduces the theory and practice of life story work – invaluable if you want to pursue this further.

Boss, P (2006) *Loss, trauma and resilience: therapeutic work with ambiguous loss*. London: Norton.

This book is useful in terms of both theory and practice in relation to ambiguous loss and resilience. It draws upon a basis in family stress theory and relates to a North American context. One drawback is that there are few links made to the work of other leading theorists in the field, despite clear areas of common ground.

Lloyd, M (2002) A framework for working with loss (Chapter 14), in Thompson, N (ed). *Loss and grief*. Basingstoke: Palgrave.

If you read nothing else on this topic, you should read this short chapter that gives an excellent overview in relation to using models of grief in the context of social work practice in the UK.

Thompson, S (2002) Older people (Chapter 11) in Thompson, N (ed). *Loss and grief*. Basingstoke: Palgrave.

Sapey, B (2002) Disability (Chapter 9) in Thompson, N (ed). *Loss and grief*. Basingstoke: Palgrave.

This overall text has already been recommended, but these two chapters are particularly relevant to some of the material in this chapter.

Chapter 5
Effective social work in response to loss and grief

Introduction

This chapter looks at the social work response at times of loss and grief. This will often be within multi-disciplinary settings, and so it is important for you, as a social worker, to be clear about your own role and skills (Currer, 2002). Lloyd (2002) identifies uncertainty about professional identity as one of the aspects of work with loss that gives rise to tensions for social workers. This chapter will therefore ask what areas are shared and which may be more distinctive. We will also consider the issue of how workers avoid or deny acknowledgement of loss, and why. Confidence about what we can offer is essential to good practice; so too are a knowledge of the other resources and agencies in our particular area of work, and good supervision and support, which together form the basis for reflective practice. The issue of how we manage personal/professional boundaries in the light of an awareness of our own losses was one that was considered in Chapter 1; it is appropriate that we should return to it here at the end of the book. Firstly, we consider a range of possible responses in the face of loss.

A range of responses

Counselling

Following Freud and the growth of what Seale (1998) refers to as the *psi-sciences*, it is common to think of the appropriate response to loss and grief as some form of counselling. Walter (1994) has suggested that the psi-sciences or psychological sciences have become seen as the experts in relation to grieving in the current period, which he labels *late modern* (but which others call *postmodern*), replacing the Church and Medicine as the authorities on these matters. Aspects of psychological approaches have become popularised through magazines and other sources to such an extent that they offer all of us, to different degrees, ways of thinking about and even constructing our 'selves'. The idea that counselling may be necessary when people grieve has grown in popularity. For example, Worden's (1991) book on the tasks of mourning is entitled *Grief counselling and grief therapy*, whilst Colin Murray Parkes is closely associated with the voluntary organisation CRUSE, which offers bereavement care and a form of counselling by volunteers.

Counselling *involves a paid or voluntary worker offering explicitly to give time, space, care and attention which focuses upon the concerns of another – the client* (Collins, 2000, p75). There is a wide range of approaches to counselling, based upon different theoretical frameworks, but all of them involve this dedicated setting aside of time, and an exclusive focus. For much of the early history of social work, some form of 'counselling' was seen to be an essential part of the role. Then this perception began to shift. In a major review of the role of social workers, the Barclay Report commented in 1982 that

> it may seem strange that we consider that we need to justify the direct counselling role
> of social workers ... we believe it is essential that social workers continue to be able to
> provide counselling ... such work is always part of assessment. (Barclay, 1982, p41)

By the 1990s, with major changes in legislation, the social worker's role had become more bureaucratic. Most social workers are no longer involved in direct work with service users and might be responsible for identifying a need for counselling but not offering it themselves. Further, there have been some writers who have been sceptical of the effectiveness of such interventions (Sheldon, 1986).

One of the effects of such debates about the place of counselling within social work is that some social workers have felt that responding to grief is not part of their job; it is something 'specialist' – either for a limited number of social workers in specialist jobs, or for 'counsellors'. This rests on two misconceptions.

- That social work no longer includes the use of counselling skills. Thompson reviews the argument that *the heart has gone out of social work* (2000, p170) and argues that we should not exaggerate the change in the basic orientation of social work. His review concludes that one of the main dangers of this position is that the issue of loss will not be addressed by social workers, when it should and must be included in every area of work. In fact, the skill base of social work is very broad, and an element of counselling is one of a range of possible methods of intervention used by social workers (Thompson, 2000, p66). Collins (2000, p7) also argues that counselling skills are used by social workers, although often in combination with other techniques and not in a 'pure' form.

- That the *only* response to loss and grief issues is 'counselling'. This is itself a very narrow view, and not one that is adopted in specialist settings such as hospices, where a range of methods is used. There are many responses in situations of loss and grief, as we shall see in the next activity. Some such techniques were mentioned in the last chapter when we considered working with children. It is not only with children, however, that we need to consider a wide repertoire of responses to grief and loss.

Other responses

The next activity asks you to identify a variety of ways of working with people experiencing loss and grief. Like some of the activities earlier in this book, it asks you to consider your own reactions following a loss, something that may be painful for you, but which will help you to think about different ways of helping other people.

ACTIVITY 5.1

Think of as many different ways of working with grief as you can. It might help to start from your own experience of grieving, or that of a friend.

- *What responses have helped you?*
- *What do you do when you visit a friend who has experienced loss?*
- *Could these approaches be used (perhaps in an adapted form) in a social work or social care setting? Why? Why not?*

Comment

There are many possible experiences that may have come to mind – perhaps what you valued most was the friend who made a meal, or the person who offered to take the children out so that you could cry in peace. Not all of these approaches can be easily adapted to fit within a professional relationship, although this will depend upon the agency and the limits of your role. Some possible responses that can be used in some settings include the following.

Touch and non-verbal responses

Our first reaction to loss in a close friend is probably to give them a hug. Touch is an important way of responding non-verbally. However, not everyone likes to be touched, particularly by someone who is not close in a personal sense, and child care workers will be aware of many caveats about the use of touch with children who may have experienced abuse. Nonetheless, touch remains an important means of conveying comfort and concern – in professional as well as personal settings. Aromatherapy involves touch as well as smell, and is increasingly used in therapeutic settings such as hospitals or hospices.

Although the use of touch may not be a feature of your role, we should be aware of its importance for those experiencing loss. 'Who gives you a hug?' may be a revealing question to ask, and we should not underestimate the comfort of physical contact. It is easy to forget the obvious – a bereaved widow may well be glad of hugs from children and grandchildren. We often speak of a pet as offering 'companionship', and should remember that a pet may also be something to hug. Both Kübler-Ross and Kessler (2005) and Payne et al. (1999) include in their books on loss sections about sexuality and the way in which this is a feature of grieving. Whilst some people find that grief kills sexual feelings, others seek the comfort that it may offer. This is an area where there may be misunderstanding between sexual partners at times of loss. Physical contact and physical forms of expression also form part of the rituals of mourning in some cultures, perhaps of some known to you.

CASE STUDY

Shameem Khan's baby died shortly after birth. The nursing staff were upset for her but unable to speak her language. Most responded by smiling uncertainly and looking away due to their uncertainty about her customs and their own embarrassment and fear of 'getting it wrong'.

Interviewed some years later, Shameem recalled one unknown female nurse who came up to her, placed her hand gently on her arm, led her to a chair and held her hand whilst she cried. No words were spoken, but this gesture transformed the entire situation for Shameem.

Sharing memories – reminiscence and the use of photographs

Another common response to loss is to look together at photographs. Berman (1993) has written about the ways in which photographs can be used in therapy. I have sometimes used this as an exercise in class, inviting students to bring a photograph of something or someone that has been 'lost'. This might be a person, or a house that they have moved from, or a pet. This is then used as the basis for sharing the experience with a fellow student. Most have found that the use of a photograph has helped both the person who is listening and the one who is talking. The situation and the loss become more 'real' for both parties, and some things are remembered that are very significant – such as the clothes someone wore, or their changing hairstyle. Photographs are often taken at happy times, such as holidays, and can help us to recall times that were shared. Scrapbooks containing photographs and mementoes can also combine different aspects. This is a way to keep special things, as well as being something that can be actively created and then shared with others. It is rather like the 'memory box' mentioned in the last chapter.

Following any loss, we need to make decisions about how that person or place will become an ongoing part of our life: this may be through photographs or memorabilia. You may find that asking a service user about how their memories will be stored and used gives them a way to think about 'relocation'. In America, some people who know they are dying make a video or DVD for their relatives to view, perhaps with special messages to be played on future occasions – like a daughter's marriage, for example. The charity Winston's Wish, mentioned in the last chapter, has – at the time of writing – created an on-line 'skyscape of memories' which is an interactive web feature on which children can post memories, including photographs, of a person who has died. Such technology is an extension of the album of faded pictures that an older person might invite you to look at. It is now customary for a hospital to invite parents to take a picture of their stillborn child – this may be their only memory of a life that was hardly lived. Life story work involves the systematic building up of a record that contains pictures as well as words (see Further Reading at the end of the last chapter).

Drawing

Drawing is another way of expressing feelings. It is most commonly used with children, but can be a good way of working with adults too. Most adults are very shy of expressing themselves in this way, but it is surprising how a drawing can sometimes be more expressive than words. Jennings and Minde (1994) write about art therapy, which is a specialised skill, but you might just find that it is helpful to ask someone to draw how they are feeling. When I have done this with a class of students, everyone usually starts by grumbling or laughing, but those who engage with it are surprised by how much the results tell us about experiencing grief. The image of being crushed under a great weight, or enveloped in a dark cloud, can offer a graphic representation, and by externalising that feeling (putting it on paper, however badly), it can become more bearable.

Writing

When someone has gone, people are often left with things that they wish they had said – writing a letter to the person can be another very useful way of expressing feelings. Putting together a diary can also be helpful. 'Narrative therapy' is a technique that was referred to in Chapter 3. Neimeyer and Anderson (2002) describe studies by Pennebaker in which people have experienced improvements in mood and even in health following being invited to write freely about their deepest feelings after a trauma or loss. The beneficial effects were experienced even when the accounts are destroyed (by agreement) without being read by anyone else – it seems to be the writing down that is important. Letter writing is something that is referred to by Kübler-Ross and Kessler (2005) as a means of externalising loss and also charting our journey through grief. It can offer a form of companionship and a practical way of continuing the bond with the person we miss. This is not restricted to situations of death, but can offer a means of expression at other times of loss too.

Bibliotherapy

Bibliotherapy refers to the therapeutic use of literature. The use of stories as a means of conveying feelings is very old – Alida Gersie (1991) has written about the myths and stories that are to be found in various cultures concerning bereavement. Reading such fables or stories can be helpful in a wide range of loss situations, and may involve referring to books that can be therapeutic for an individual (Jones, 2001) or can aid the use of stories in group settings. In relation to the latter, Gersie (1997) has explored dimensions of the group experience (such as gender and class) in work with people of all ages and in different settings. There may then be activities associated with hearing the story, perhaps in a group context. Howie (1983) has written an account of the way in which this technique has been used during a club for people who are depressed. Again the use of a story can open up emotions and help people to reflect upon and maybe talk about their feelings.

Music and movement

You may also have considered the power of music or of movement in both expressing and responding to loss. The use of the creative arts in health and social care is growing, having been neglected for too long. Ruth Bright, who has written one of the key texts on grief (1996), is a music therapist and gives illustrations of the ways in which music can be used. Aldridge (2000) also demonstrates the use of music in care settings, whilst Warren (1993) and Payne (1993) are useful sources on the creative arts generally, and Payne (1990) and Levy (1995) are particularly informative about dance therapy. Jennings (1998) also offers an introduction to drama therapy.

Implications for social work

No-one is suggesting that you become an expert drama or music therapist, but it is important that you are aware of the range of techniques and approaches that may be helpful at times of loss. 'Talking therapies' – such as counselling – do not represent the full range of approaches that can be of value in working with people experiencing loss. Whilst less verbal approaches may be particularly suitable in daycare or residential settings with service users who find verbal expression difficult (such as children, people with some form of learning disability, or older people with dementia), their use is not restricted to such groups or settings. English culture is one that relies heavily on verbal expression – but use of the other senses and of other forms of expression can be especially powerful for all groups. Physical activities do not have to involve explicit therapy – a local line-dancing class was the therapy of choice for one woman following a serious loss, for example, whilst another took up swimming. These are all ways of re-engaging with life after loss, and regaining a sense of agency.

Working in partnership

Just as there is a division of labour within social care, with direct work usually falling to those in residential or daycare settings, so clearly there are different workers involved with those who use services. Increasingly, boundaries have become blurred in some settings. Communication is fundamental to all work in human services, and most people who work in health or social care utilise some kind of counselling or listening skills. This is also true of those in the voluntary services.

The next activity explores these issues in relation to your own area of practice, or one well known to you.

ACTIVITY **5.2**

List all the people in your team, making a note of their professional role or title. Include yourself. In relation to a service user experiencing loss or grief, how do you think their responses would differ from each other and why?

Comment

This activity offers a simple way of starting to think about your own working situation, and is likely to draw your attention to some issues in relation to it. It may be that you did not find it easy to define the boundaries of your 'team'. In some areas of work, this is clearer than others. Does it include those with whom you work every day, or others with whom you may interact less frequently? The 'team' may be different in relation to different service users. If this is the case, you may wish to draw up a list in relation to a defined service user or series of common situations that are part of your work. Or perhaps you work in a more clearly defined situation. Have you included administrative colleagues in your list? So the first point to note is that the very idea of a 'team' may be both negotiable and shifting.

However you have defined your 'team', you might then like to think about the different aspects of loss that the team encounters. For example, you might work in a children's disability team. Here there may be bereavement when a seriously disabled child dies, but also the grief on the part of parents that is involved in learning of a child's disability, and the ongoing struggles of living with this on a daily basis. Grief recurs at different stages; when the child cannot start at a local school, for example. Families (including siblings) experience many losses as a result of such a situation.

Next, there are different roles to consider. Senior staff may be responsible for procedures, budgeting, and liaison with managers in other services, as well as supervision. Even at this level, somewhat removed from the service user, knowledge of the effects of grief and of the importance of this issue is vitally important if it is to be incorporated within procedures and acknowledged as a crucial staff issue.

Other team members will be in direct contact with the family. Depending upon your area of practice, these may be social workers, nurses, teachers, family support workers, home care assistants and administrators who answer the telephone. They may not expect to do 'counselling' in any pure sense. But they do all need to be able to listen sensitively to strong and troubled feelings, and to refer on appropriately. Some team members may have 'hands on' contact with service users, attending to physical care needs such as bathing.

It is vitally important that everyone involved is alert to expressions of grief, and should respond appropriately at the time, being careful not to dismiss or belittle feelings. But it is also important to recognise that practical help is an appropriate and often valuable response in situations of loss. One study (Currer, 2001) of the writings of people who were dying suggested that they needed to attend to three concerns:

- abandoning the future;

- managing the present;

- renegotiating relationships.

This might be applied to other situations of impending or current loss. The first aspect may involve helping a person to find meaning in their situation. This links to the 'stages of dying' described in Chapter 3, and may involve the use of counselling skills in some form. But meanwhile, there are also practical current difficulties to be dealt with. This is not quite the same as the distinction between 'loss orientation' and 'restoration orientation' because in a situation of future or current turmoil and loss, the idea of restoration is not relevant. It is more about getting through the day-to-day. If increasing physical illness is involved (as it is for people who are dying) or ongoing physical difficulties (as may be the case when someone is elderly or in situations of disability), this task of managing the everyday is enormous. Help with this is a real contribution to facing loss. The final aspect of helping people to renegotiate relationships with others as they adapt to changed situations may also be a part of the role of the team in different ways.

In health and social care settings generally, the responses of those involved with a particular family will vary for many reasons. Firstly, their role and level of involvement are different. Their training and professional backgrounds are varied. There are also likely to be differences of gender, age, and maybe ethnicity. And there will be personal differences – for example, one team member may him or herself have had an experience that is close to that of the service user group – as well as personality differences. This is a rich mix, which can be used creatively by the team if it is acknowledged and if all contributions are valued, within an overall shared understanding of the effects of grieving and the needs of families and a common commitment to working with issues of grief and loss.

It is likely that some of the services needed in a situation of loss cannot be provided from within any particular team. Part of working in a multi-disciplinary way is to be aware of the local services that are available, including those in the voluntary sector. It is also important to know not only what services exist and how these can be accessed, but also about the level of training of their workers and their limitations. For example, CRUSE Bereavement Care is a specialist voluntary agency with local branches in many areas (but not all). They only accept self-referrals, which means that the service user must ring the helpline him or herself. They do not offer an emergency or out of hours service; there may be an answerphone and someone will ring back. It would be important for you and the service user to know this. The Samaritans, on the other hand, do offer a listening service at any time. CRUSE workers are local volunteers. Although trained to a certain level, they are not accredited counsellors. They have not been trained to deal with complicated mental health issues. Sometimes voluntary agencies feel that professional workers use them as a 'dumping ground' when they are at a loss as to what else to suggest. It is important for service users that referrals to other services are well informed and make good use of scarce resources. Finally, it should go without saying that the crucial partnership is that which is established with service users and carers as the service seeks to identify and respond to their needs.

I referred above to the different roles of team members. We turn next to look at what is, or should be, characteristic of the social work role in relation to working with people experiencing loss of various kinds.

The social work role

In a multi-disciplinary team, we need to be aware of areas where the remit for different professionals may overlap. It is also important to be clear about the ways in which one's own role is distinct. In relation to social work, Parton argues that:

> ... *defining the nature, boundaries and settings of social work, as distinct from other practices, has always been difficult ... social work is in an essentially contested and ambiguous position.* (Parton, 1996, p6)

This ambiguity is as great at present as it has been for the last 30 years, since the large social services departments that were once the major vehicles for statutory social work intervention are being dismantled. Structures now mirror the long-stated aim of multi-disciplinary work with either health or education. Meanwhile, the nursing role has expanded to encompass many aspects of what used to be social work. As already seen, in 1982 the Barclay Report argued that social work was to include a 'counselling role', together with practical assistance with matters such as benefits. Studying social work intervention following the Hillsborough disaster, Newburn found that it was the *combination of practical and emotional support* that was valued by service users, and analysis suggests (Currer, 2001, p19) that it is this combination of emotional care with practical assistance that gives social work its particular character. (In a similar way, nursing care combines emotional with physical care.) In different work settings, these elements may be combined in different proportions – and there may be other features also. Of course, the actual work will be dictated by statutory requirements in many cases.

A few years ago, I undertook a study (Currer, 2001) in which I asked social workers working with people who were experiencing bereavement in specialist and mainstream settings about the key elements of their work. The following are the three features that were identified by them.

- **Recognising and endorsing the need to grieve**. This may be as simple as stopping by the chair of an elderly resident who is crying, for example.

- **Accompaniment in grief**. This is most likely to be a feature of long-term involvement; there are many ways to convey that one is 'alongside', as we shall see below.

- **Support in relation to questions about re-engagement**. As we have seen, Stroebe and Schut suggest that 'restoration' is ongoing throughout the grieving process. Social workers may have a particular role in supporting attempts at restoration through re-engagement, or in helping with early activities that are necessary in times of loss.

These features are not in themselves particular to social work, but within each, there will be both an emotional and a practical element. They may seem rather obvious, but this can be used as a way of thinking about the various responses that may be needed from social workers in very different roles and settings.

The next activity asks you to think of some specific examples from settings familiar to you.

ACTIVITY 5.3

Choose two contrasting social work roles – perhaps working with different client groups, in residential or field care. Within each:

- *identify a loss that a service user may be experiencing – you may find it useful to look back at the situations of loss in social work that you identified in Chapter 1.*

- *then give illustrations of each of the three features outlined above from each situation. Make a note of your responses.*

Comment

The roles and losses that you have identified will depend upon the nature of your own social work experience. My comments focus upon the second part of the activity.

- Recognising or endorsing the need to grieve can be very simple, involving only an acknowledgement of the loss that has occurred. This sounds very simple, yet it is something that we often fail to do, for reasons that will be explored further below. In a residential setting, it may involve noticing that someone is upset, and treating this seriously. In a very different setting, one emergency duty worker told of the situation of an elderly woman without sight whose daughter (also her carer) had died in the house. The social worker, who had been called in to arrange for alternative accommodation for the mother, had to delay police and others who wanted to remove the body, giving the blind woman a chance first to say 'goodbye' to her daughter by touching her face. This recognition of the importance of taking just a moment to grieve was deeply unpopular with the others involved, but absolutely crucial for the older woman. If we consider the Dual Process Model of Stroebe and Schut (see Chapter 3), we can see that some people focus upon 'restoration' at the expense of giving time to their loss and the need to grieve, which may be because they have responsibilities for others. As professionals, we are sometimes in the position of 'giving permission' for grief, something that connects with 'loss orientation'. This can involve 'stopping the action' and challenging the tendency of other people to move on. Elsewhere, I have used examples that illustrate this in the case of bereavement both in a hospital and a community setting (Currer, 2001, p141f). In a daycare setting, putting grief and loss on the agenda as topics for discussion is another way in which they can be endorsed and recognised at a group level, so that when a loss occurs, it is a subject that can be raised with the minimum of embarrassment.

- Accompaniment in grief is likely to be a feature of long-term involvement. If we have known the service user before the loss occurred, we may be able to share with them memories of a time before it happened, or to encourage them to reflect upon how their feelings have perhaps become less painful over time, or how well they have 'coped'. This aspect involves the first, since accompaniment can only begin when the grief or loss is mutually recognised. This accompaniment is not counselling – you can perhaps think of good friends with whom you have occasional contact (perhaps a card or phone call) but who have been 'with you' through difficult times, checking out how things are going or remembering key dates or anniversaries. Accompaniment can sometimes be more practical – going with someone to a special place such as a graveside, or the street where a child first lived or went to school. Sometimes it just means hearing the story over and over again. Working with carers, accompaniment might mean facilitating a break from care.

- Support in relation to re-engagement requires considerable sensitivity. It has obvious connections with Stroebe and Schut's 'restoration orientation'. As they have pointed out, this is not an 'end point' of grief, but an ongoing process. There are practical demands that begin immediately after any loss – after all, loss involves change, and often this needs an immediate response, long before the person is ready for it. This aspect also has close links to the practical aspect of the social work role, and to the social dimension of it. Writing as a specialist social worker, Monroe (1998) identifies a number of features of social work in palliative care. Intervention will include information giving; helping communication and freeing up people's confidence to act, sometimes through helping with resources.

You may recall that Stroebe and Schut had suggested that 'normal' grieving is charac-terised by an oscillation between the loss and a restoration orientation. That is, people commonly move between acknowledging and focusing upon their loss and concentrating upon the future, often in practical ways. In different ways, the three aspects of the social work role identified above can support each of these two orientations. It is important, however, to realise that this sort of oscillation can occur in the space of a day. Thompson and Thompson (1999) give the example of an older person who was consumed with grief when something reminded him of how much he misses his dead wife, and then later in the day was much happier when he was working in the garden with some plants that she had loved. The authors warn that it would be possible for a worker who was conducting an assessment of his needs to have a false impression of his mental state depending upon when they called to see him, if they were to generalise from this.

Denial of loss

Recognising grief – why we avoid it

I have suggested that the first of the three features of work with those experiencing loss is one that is frequently avoided. In this section, we consider the ways in which social work-ers (together with many others) avoid recognising grief, and also look at the reasons for this. We need to be very specific if we are to identify bad practices and habits that often become so routinised that they are invisible to us. Try to do this activity yourself with the commentary covered up – you will find it useful to be able to compare your own responses to those reported here.

ACTIVITY **5.4**

Focus upon a practice situation familiar to you.

- *List the ways in which social workers avoid recognising grief and distress in service users. Be very specific – examples might be 'not making eye contact' or 'looking at your watch'. Think of ways that are individual and also perhaps some ways in which the structure or organisation of services serves the same purpose – for example, through staff changes or expecting people to talk to different people.*

- *Now list some possible reasons why this happens, in your view.*

Comment

The following table gives responses to this activity from other students. You might have noted some different ones. Each service setting varies from the next, and there are no final answers. The responses are put together from two cohorts of students who came from a variety of practice backgrounds – your list is likely to be much shorter.

How we avoid or deny grief	Reasons for denying grief
Focus upon the practical at the expense of the emotional	We may feel responsible
Offer to make a cup of tea	Fear of opening the floodgates (practical or emotional)
Stop listening; switch off; change the subject	Fear that we can't deal with it
Do not ask about it	Sense of our own inadequacy
Refer on; pass the buck	It is not within our job description
Make a joke	It is not a departmental priority
'I hear what you are saying'	Genuine pressure of other work
Say we have another appointment	Concern that we may do more harm
Gloss over it, offer reassurance	It touches our own losses too closely
Focus upon the positive	It is the end of the day
Deny responsibility	We are stressed
Do not ask questions about unusual behaviour	We do not even see the grief due to our false assumptions
Shift changes	We do not really care
	Fear of stepping on the toes of another worker

This activity is reminiscent of Activity 1.5, in Chapter 1 (see page 20), when you thought of situations for which workers might be seen to be responsible. You may have been responsible for arranging a place in a residential care home for someone who was reluctant to go. We have already suggested in the last chapter that this may for many people seem like a form of 'social death', the beginning of the end. Yet it may have involved considerable negotiation on your part. It is very discouraging when the person concerned can only see the loss involved, and it would be very natural to encourage them to look at the positives. Yet this is a loss, and it may mean a great deal if you can acknowledge this. Some mothers (sadly, not all) who have experienced social workers removing their children from home comment upon the humanity and sympathy with which this difficult task has been done. For some this may be irrelevant, but for others, we know that some acknowledgement of their pain can make an intolerable situation better. It is important that our own guilt and doubt do not get in the way.

Did you notice that only one of the examples above (shift changes) could be called 'structural'? In fact, there are many aspects of the ways in which services are arranged or structured that can be seen as a defence against the tendency for powerful emotions to explode. Staff may retreat to a separate 'staff room', for example. This was first formally recognised in a classic paper by Menzies (1959). Isabel Menzies studied the working patterns of nurses, and described the variety of distancing strategies used by them to protect themselves from the emotional impact of their work.

Turning to the reasons listed, we need to remember that some of them are perfectly legitimate. We do have to be aware of the limits of our own role and responsibilities; it is no help to service users if we are not clear about this. We also have to be sure of our own skills and confident about what we are doing, insofar as this is possible, finding other ways to deal with our own inevitable anxiety and distress. Yet an acknowledgement of grief may not take long or be as demanding as we fear. It is a lot kinder to say 'I realise this is very hard for you' than to pretend we have not noticed. Sometimes, we do indeed need to move the intervention on, to focus upon the practical or the positive.

Supervision

Reflective practice – our own experience of loss: burn-out and supervision

Reflective practice involves the ability to look at why we are acting in a certain way, and to identify patterns of action or response that are more about our own needs than those of service users. Look back at Activity 1.7 in Chapter 1 (see p23), where you considered your own areas of strength and vulnerability, and at Activity 1.8 (p25), where you looked at the system of supervision that operates in your own workplace. Many of the fears identified in the lists following Activity 5.4 relate to difficulties that we may have in coping with the grief of others if we have not recognised our own losses and developed ways of dealing with these.

There is a tension at the heart of social work between 'being yourself' and being professional. This was recognised very early by one of the first writers to define the values of social work (Biestek, 1961). One of the principles that this author wrote about was 'controlled emotional involvement'. This is about our ability to acknowledge feelings and respond sensitively, whilst also standing outside and retaining control in situations that often feel out of control (Thompson, 2000, p108). This is often very much valued by service users (Newburn, 1993). Crying together may have a place, but we are employed to go beyond this as well. This tension is hard to maintain. Workers in situations such as hospices know that maintaining the balance between being affected emotionally themselves and being able to stand apart is one of their key skills. It is for this reason that supervision structures are in place to support workers as well as service users.

Once again, it is worth noting that the techniques for maintaining personal integrity and this difficult balance may be structural as much as personal. Supervision has been referred to already, but this is not the only protection against 'burn-out' in workers. In a study of nurses working in London on a ward for cancer patients, Katz (1989) suggests that the congruence (or lack of it) between ideology and structure is important in preventing stress for nurses. What she means by this is that workers have an idea about what constitutes good practice for them (ideology). Some work structures are such that good practice is facilitated; in others the structure seems to prevent good practice. Even in situations where the nature of the work is inherently stressful, workers will survive (and thrive) where there is harmony (or 'congruence') between these elements, but will suffer stress and burn-out if this is not the case. I have found that Katz's observations from this study of nurses rings many bells for social workers in a range of service areas, particularly at times when such services are changing rapidly so that their structures do not seem to support good practice. Certainly this would account for the sense of work satisfaction that is often reported in hospice situations, where structures and rituals are often in place to support a commonly agreed ideology of care.

The issue of resource constraints is also one that needs to be acknowledged. Again, workers are often frustrated by their inability to provide services when these are clearly needed. Honesty is essential, and it is possible in some instances to share this frustration with service users, fighting restrictions and limits insofar as this is possible. Sometimes workers are faced with a choice between loyalty to the organisation and loyalty to the service user in terms of acknowledging the limitations of systems and policies. No training can 'tell you what to do' in such difficult situations, but it is important that you are honest with yourself about the issues, and do not get into the habit of defensive practice that denies – implicitly or explicitly – the reality of the needs that you observe. Being clear about your own losses and agendas is part of this difficult equation. Supervision should be a place where these and other tensions can be acknowledged openly. If they are not, the service will experience spiralling sickness rates as individual workers pay an individual price for political inadequacies.

Supervision should be a mechanism whereby workers can feel trusted, supported and valued (Thompson, 2000). According to Morrison (1993), it may also offer opportunities for:

- staff development, through the promotion of ongoing learning;
- staff care, by protecting staff from harmful aspects of work – this may include the offer of additional opportunities for confidential counselling;
- arbitration and mediation if conflicts and difficulties arise.

In order to get the most from supervision, Thompson suggests that workers need to be:

- honest – with themselves and each other;
- prepared – in order to make the best use of limited time;
- assertive – making supervision work is a joint responsibility.

(Thompson, 2000, p147)

The critical social work practitioner

What sort of practitioner are you? Adams et al. (2002) suggest that it is crucial that social workers are 'critical' practitioners. This does not mean that they are always complaining – far from it. Being a critical practitioner involves being up to date with theoretical understandings and models, and confident in using these appropriately. It involves self-awareness, and the ability to reflect upon one's own practice. It can involve challenging policy and practice from a sound and thoughtful basis. Above all, it involves keeping the service user and their needs always at the centre of the picture, and using our considerable power and resources (which often do not feel as if they are sufficient) in their interests. As we have discussed, supervision can play a crucial role in sustaining your ability to be a critical and pro-active practitioner.

ACTIVITY 5.5

Bearing in mind the description of a critical practitioner, make a note of the things that you remember from this book that will enhance your practice.

Then make a separate note of areas in which you feel you need to do more reading, or more thinking.

Finally, note the aspects of your current workplace that seem to hinder creative work with the loss and grief that service users are experiencing. What, if anything, can be done to change them? What do you need from others if you are to offer the best possible service, and what do you need to do yourself?

Whatever your area of practice, it will involve working with loss and grief. You do not need to have all the answers, as the following extract from a book about suicide suggests:

> You need to know that, as a helper, you do not have to fix things up for people. Survivors need help in working out their answers. Ultimately, it is their answers that are the only ones that are not totally irrelevant. (Lukas and Sieden, 1990, pp146–7)

You do need to be prepared, however, to stay with the pain while people work towards their own solutions, and to be aware of some resources – which should include your knowledge of relevant theories and models – and able to use these creatively in the context of a positive and affirming relationship.

C   H   A   P   T   E   R   S   U   M   M   A   R   Y

This chapter began by questioning the idea that formal counselling is the only possible practice response in situations of loss and grief. We considered:

- a range of non-verbal and other interventions that have been found helpful;

- aspects of responding to loss within a multi-disciplinary team setting;

- the nature of the social work response, and three key features of this;

- reasons why it may be hard for workers to acknowledge the grief of service users, and the practical ways in which this may be denied;

- the tension that may exist between using ourselves and our human responses, and staying objective in order to help a service user who feels helpless in the face of grief;

- the importance of supervision and structural factors in helping us to be reflective and critical practitioners, and in protecting workers from stress and burn-out.

FURTHER READING

Currer, C (2001) *Responding to grief: dying, bereavement and social care*. Basingstoke: Palgrave.

Whilst this book is specifically about dying and bereavement, rather than loss more broadly, it is written for social workers in both specialist and mainstream settings, and identifies key features of the social work role, with illustrations from practice.

Thompson, N (2000) *Understanding social work*. Basingstoke: Palgrave.

This basic introduction to social work includes comments on the place of counselling skills, and also the importance of supervision.

Bright, R (1996) *Grief and powerlessness*. London: Jessica Kingsley.

This book is included here because of its references to music therapy. It is a useful all-round text and was recommended following Chapter 1 for this reason.

Howie, M (1983) Bibliotherapy in social work. *British Journal of Social Work*, 13: 287–309.

Although now rather old, this paper outlines and illustrates the use of bilbiotherapy in a group for elderly depressed patients.

Conclusion

I said at the outset that I hoped to convince you of the importance of the study of loss and grief within social work and of the interest that this subject holds. Only you can say if this has been the case. Yet if it is to serve its purpose of enhancing social work practice, this cannot be a theoretical or abstract interest alone. The self-awareness and reflection that have been features of this book need to be evident in improving practice – through trying out new ways of working and through engagement with developing research and theory in this field. Just as you have looked in this book at recent developments in theory, so things will go on changing, and it is your responsibility to ensure that you keep up to date. Most importantly, theory needs to be built upon and to include the real experience of social work practitioners. Loss is a fascinating subject, and it is my hope that this book will have stimulated your interest so that you will go on learning and developing your practice in relation to this topic long after reaching this final page and when this book has long been out of print.

References

Abercrombie, N, Hill, S and Turner, B (eds) (1988) Custom, in *The Penguin dictionary of sociology. (2nd edition)*. Harmondsworth: Penguin.

Ablon, J (1986 [1973]) Reactions of Samoan burn patients and families to severe burns, in Currer, C and Stacey, M (eds) *Concepts of health, illness and disease*. Leamington Spa: Berg.

Adams, R, Dominelli, L and Payne, M (eds) (2002) *Critical practice in social work*. London: Palgrave.

Aldridge, D (2000) *Music therapy in dementia care*. London: Jessica Kingsley.

Antonovsky, A (1987) *Unravelling the mystery of health*. London: Jossey-Bass.

Ariès, P (1974) *Western attitudes toward death from the Middle Ages to the present*. London: Marion Boyars Publishers.

Ariès, P (1981) *The hour of our death*. London: Allen Lane.

Arroba, T and James, K (1987) *Pressure at work: A survival guide*. London: McGraw-Hill.

Attenborough, R and Eastman, B (1993) *Shadowlands* (film). Savoy Pictures.

Attig, T (2002) Relearning the world: making and finding meanings. In Neimeyer, R (ed) *Meaning reconstruction and the experience of loss*. Washington, DC: American Psychological Association.

Barclay, P (1982) *Social workers: Their roles and tasks*. London. National Institute for Social Work.

Barley, N (1995) *Dancing on the grave*. London: John Murray.

Beckett, C (2002) *Human growth and development*. London: Sage.

Beresford, P, Adshead, L and Croft, S (2007) *Palliative care, social work and service users*. London: Jessica Kingsley.

Berman, L (1993) *Beyond the smile: The therapeutic use of the photograph*. London: Routledge.

Biestek, F (1961) *The casework relationship*. London: Allen and Unwin.

Bishop, V (ed) (1997) *Clinical supervision in practice: Some questions, answers and guidelines*. London: Macmillan.

Boss, P (1999) *Ambiguous loss:Learning to live with unresolved grief*. Cambridge, MA: Harvard University Press.

Boss, P (2006) *Loss, trauma and resilience: Therapeutic work with ambiguous loss*. New York: WW Norton and Company.

Bowlby, J (1969) *Attachment and loss,* vol 1: *Attachment*. London: Hogarth Press.

Bowlby, J (1971) *Loss*. Harmondsworth: Penguin.

Bowlby, J (1973) *Attachment and loss,* vol II: *Separation: Anxiety and anger.* London: Hogarth Press.

Bowlby, J (1973) *Attachment and loss,* vol III: *Sadness and depression.* London: Hogarth Press.

Bowlby, J and Parkes, CM (1970) Separation and loss within the family, in Anthony, EJ (ed) *The child in his family*. New York: Wiley.

Bradbury, M (1993) Contemporary representations of 'good' and 'bad' death, in Dickenson, D and Johnson, M (eds) *Death, dying and bereavement*. London: Sage.

Bradbury, M (1999) *Representations of death: A social and psychological perspective*. London: Routledge.

Bright, R (1996) *Grief and powerlessness*. London: Jessica Kingsley.

Brown, G and Harris, T (1978) *The social origins of depression*. London: Tavistock.

Browne, A and Bourne, I (1996) *The social work supervisor: Supervision in community, day care and residential settings*. Buckingham: Open University Press.

Bruce, E and Schultz, C (2001) *Nonfinite loss and grief*. London: Jessica Kingsley.

Buckman, R (1998) Communication in palliative care: a practical guide, in Doyle, D et al. (eds) *Oxford Textbook of Palliative Medicine. (2nd edition)*. Oxford: Oxford University Press.

Cairney, J, Chettle, K, Clark, M (2006) Editorial. *Social Work Education*, 25 (4): 315–18.

Camus, A (1982 [1942]) *The Outsider* (trans. J. Laredo). Harmondsworth: Penguin.

Clark, D (1993) Death in Staithes, in Dickenson, D and Johnson, M (eds) *Death, dying and bereavement*. London: Sage.

Collins, S (2000) Counselling, in Davies, M (ed) *The Blackwell encyclopaedia of social work*. Oxford: Blackwell.

Corr, C (1993) Coping with dying: Lessons we should and should not learn from the work of Elisabeth Kübler-Ross. *Death Studies*, 17: 69–83.

Couldrick, A (1995) A cradling of a different sort, in Smith, S and Pennells, S M (eds) *Interventions with bereaved children*. London: Jessica Kingsley.

Cree, V (2000) *Sociology for social workers and probation officers*. London: Routledge.

Cree, V and Davis, A (2007) *Social work: Voices from the inside*. London: Routledge.

Crepet, P, Ferrari, G, Platt, S (eds) (1992) *Suicidal behaviour in Europe*. London: John Libbey and Co. Ltd.

Currer, C (2001) *Responding to grief: Dying, bereavement and social care*. Basingstoke: Palgrave.

Currer, C (2002) Dying and bereavement, in Adams, R, Dominelli, L and Payne, M (eds) *Critical practice in social work*. London: Palgrave.

Currer, C and Stacey, M (eds) (1986) *Concepts of health, illness and disease*. Leamington Spa: Berg.

Davis, A and Ellis, K (1995) Enforced altruism in community care, in Hugman, R and Smith, D (eds) *Ethical issues in social work.* London: Routledge.

DfES (2005) *Common core of skills and knowledge for the children's workforce.* Nottingham: DfES publications. Available at www.everychildmatters.gov.uk/deliveringservices/commoncore/

DfES (2007) *Annual review of the children and young people's plan (supplementary guidance).* London: The Stationery Office. Available at www.everychildmatters.gov.uk/IG00192

DoH (1999) *National Service Framework for mental health: Modern standards and service models.* London: The Stationery Office. Available at www.dh.gov.uk/en/Publicationsandstatistics/Publications/PublicationsPolicyAndGuidance/DH_4009598

DoH (2006) *A new ambition for old age: Next steps in implementing the National Service Framework for older people.* London: The Stationery Office. Available at www.dh.gov.uk/en/Publicationsandstatistics/Publications/PublicationsPolicyAndGuidance/DH_4133941

Doka, K (1989) Disenfranchised grief, in Doka, K (ed) *Disenfranchised grief: Recognising hidden sorrow.* Lexington, MA: Lexington.

Doka, K (ed) (2002) *Disenfranchised grief: New directions, challenges and strategies for practice.* Illinois: Research Press.

Durkheim, E (1951 [1897]) *Suicide: A study in sociology.* New York: Free Press.

Eisenbruch, M (1984) Cross-cultural aspects of bereavement. II Ethnic and cultural variations in the development of bereavement practices. *Culture, Medicine and Psychiatry*, 8 (4): 315–47.

Elkington, G and Harrison, G (1996) *Caring for someone at home.* Carer's National Association: Hodder and Stoughton.

Eyre, R and Wood, C (2001) *Iris* (film). Miramax Films.

Fahlberg, V (1991) *A child's journey through placement.* Indianapolis: Perspectives Press.

Field, D, Hockey, J and Small, N (eds) (1997) *Death, gender and ethnicity.* London: Routledge.

Fordham, M and Ketteridge, A-M (1998) Men must work and women must weep: examining gender stereotypes in disasters, in Enarson, E and Morrow, B (eds) *Through women's eyes: the gendered terrain of disaster.* Westport, CT: Praeger.

Fraser, M, Richman J and Galinsky, M (1999) Risk, protection, and resilience: Toward a conceptual framework for social work practice. *Social Work Research*, 23 (3): 131.

Froggatt, K (1997) Rites of passage and the hospice culture. *Mortality*, 2 (3): 123–36.

Gambe, D, Gomes, J and Kapur V (1992) *Improving practice with children and families: A training manual.* London: CCETSW.

Gersie, A (1991) *Story making in bereavement: Dragons fight in the meadow.* London: Jessica Kingsley.

Gersie, A (1997) *Reflections on therapeutic storymaking: The use of stories in groups.* London: Jessica Kingsley.

Giddens, A (1991) *Modernity and self-identity: Self and society in the late modern age.* Cambridge: Polity Press.

Gielen, U (1997) A death on the roof of the world: the perspective of Tibetan Buddhism, in Parkes, CM, Laungani, P and Young, B (eds) *Death and bereavement across cultures*. London: Routledge.

Gilliard, J (1992) A different kind of loss. *Social Work Today*, 3 December.

Glaser, B and Strauss, A (1965) *Awareness of dying*. Chicago, IL: Aldine.

Glaser, B and Strauss, A (1968) *Time for dying*. Chicago, IL: Aldine.

Goffman, E (1969) *The presentation of self in everyday life*. Harmondsworth: Penguin.

Goldsworthy, K Kellie (2005) Grief and loss theory in social work practice: All changes involve loss, just as all losses involve change. *Australian Social Work*, 58 (2): 167–78.

Gorer, G (1965) *Death, grief and mourning in contemporary Britain*. London: Cresset.

Goss, R and Klass, D (2005) *Dead but not lost*. Oxford: Altamira Press.

Gunaratnam, Y (1997) Culture is not enough: A critique of multi-culturalism in palliative care, in Field, D, Hockey, J and Small, N (eds) *Death, gender and ethnicity*. London: Routledge.

Hagman, G (2001) Beyond decathexis: Toward a new psychoanalytic understanding and treatment of mourning, in Neimeyer, R (ed) *Meaning reconstruction and the experience of loss*. Washington, DC: American Psychological Association.

Hammick, G (ed) (1992) *Love and loss*. London: Virago Press.

Harvey, J (ed) (1998) *Perspectives on loss: A sourcebook*. Philadelphia: Taylor and Francis.

Hattersley, L (1999) Trends in life expectancy by social class – an update. *Health Statistics Quarterly*, 2: 16–24. Published in web format, 5 August 2005, www.statistics.gov.uk/articles/hsq/HSQ2Life Expectancy.pdf

Hawkins, P and Shohet, R (2000) *Supervision in the helping professions. (2nd edition)*. London: Open University Press.

Hepworth, M (2000) *Stories of ageing*. Buckingham: Open University Press.

Hockey, J, Katz, J and Small, N (eds) (2001) *Grief, mourning and death ritual*. Buckingham: Open University Press.

Holloway, M (2007a) *Negotiating death in contemporary health and social care*. Bristol: Policy Press.

Holloway, M (2007b) Spiritual need and the core business of social work. *British Journal of Social Work*, 37: 265–80.

Holmes, T and Rahé, R (1967) The social readjustment rating scale. *Journal of Psychosomatic Research*, 11: 213–8.

Hooyman, N and Kramer, B (2006) *Living through loss:Interventions across the life span*. New York: Columbia University Press.

Howarth, G (2007) *Death and dying*. Cambridge: Polity Press.

Howe, D (1995) *Attachment theory for social work practice*. London: Macmillan.

Howe, D, Sawbridge, P and Hinings, D (1992) *Half a million women*. Penguin: Harmondsworth.

Howie, M (1983) Bibliotherapy in social work. *British Journal of Social Work*, 13: 287–309.

Ironside, V (1996) *You'll get over it: The rage of bereavement.* Harmondsworth: Penguin.

Jennings, S (1998) *Introduction to dramatherapy.* London: Jessica Kingsley

Jennings, S and Minde, A (1994) *Art therapy and drama therapy: Masks of the soul.* London: Jessica Kingsley.

Jewett, C (1984) *Helping children cope with separation and loss.* London: Batsford with BAAF.

Jones, E (2001) *Bibliotherapy for bereaved children.* London: Jessica Kingsley.

Katz, J (1989) Context and care: nurses' accounts of stress and support on a cancer ward. Unpublished PhD Thesis, Department of Sociology, University of Warwick.

Keenan, B (1994) *An evil cradling: The five year ordeal of a hostage.* Harmondsworth: Penguin.

Keith, L (1994) *Mustn't grumble.* London: The Women's Press.

Kellehear, A (1990) *Dying of cancer: The final year of life.* London: Harwood Academic.

Klass, D, Silverman, P and Nickman, S (eds) (1996) *Continuing bonds: New understandings of grief.* Philadelphia: Taylor and Francis.

Kroll, B (1994) *Chasing rainbows: Children, loss and divorce.* London: Jessica Kingsley.

Kroll, B (2002) Children and divorce, in Thompson, N (ed) *Loss and grief.* Basingstoke: Palgrave.

Kübler-Ross, E (1970) *On death and dying.* London: Tavistock.

Kübler- Ross, E and Kessler, D (2005) *On grief and grieving.* London: Simon and Schuster.

Lazarus, R and Folkman, S (1984) *Stress, appraisal and coping.* New York: Springer-Verlag.

Lepper, J (2007) Healing the hurt. *Children Now*, 21–27 March, 31-2. Available at www.childrennow.co.uk

Levine, E (1997) Jewish views and customs on death, in Parkes, CM, Laungani, P and Young, B (eds) *Death and bereavement across cultures.* London: Routledge.

Levy, F (ed) (1995) *Dance and other expressive art therapies.* London: Routledge.

Lewis, CS (1961) *A grief observed.* London: Faber and Faber.

Lindemann, E (1994 [1944]) Symptomatology and management of acute grief. *American Journal of Psychiatry*, 151 (6): 155–60 (50th anniversary reprint from original article).

Lishman, J (1998) Personal and professional development, in Adams, R, Dominelli, L and Payne, M (eds) *Social work: themes, issues and debates.* London: Macmillan.

Lister, L (1991) Men and grief: a review of research. *Smith College Studies in Social Work*, 61: 220–35.

Littlewood, J (1993) The denial of death and rites of passage in contemporary societies, in Clark, D (ed) *The sociology of death.* Oxford: Blackwell.

Lloyd, M (2002) A framework for working with loss, in Thompson, N (ed) *Loss and grief.* Basingstoke: Palgrave.

Lukas, C and Sieden, H (1990) *Silent grief: Living in the wake of suicide*. London: Macmillan.

Mallon, B (1998) *Helping children to manage loss*. London: Jessica Kingsley.

Marris, P (1982) Attachment and society, in Parkes, CM and Stevenson-Hinde, J (eds) *The place of attachment in human behaviour*. London: Tavistock.

Marris, P (1986) *Loss and change (revised edition)* London: Routledge

Marris, P (1991) The social construction of uncertainty, in Parkes, CM et al. (eds) *Attachment across the life cycle*. London: Routledge.

Menzies, I (1959) The functioning of social systems as a defence against anxiety: A report on a study of the nursing service of a general hospital. *Human Relations*, 13: 95–121.

Middleton, J (1982) Lugbara death, in Bloch, M and Parry, J (eds) *Death and the regeneration of life*. Cambridge: Cambridge University Press.

Monroe, B (1998) Social work in palliative care, in Doyle, D, Hanks, G and MacDonald, N (eds) *The Oxford handbook of palliative care*. Oxford: Oxford University Press.

Moore, O (1996) *PWA*. London: Picador.

Morrison, T (1993) *Supervision in social care*. Harlow: Longman.

Mulkay, M and Ernst, J (1991) The changing profile of social death. *Archives of European Sociology*, 32: 172–96.

Neimeyer, R (2000) Searching for the meaning of meaning. *Death Studies*, 24: 541–58.

Neimeyer, R (ed) (2001) *Meaning reconstruction and the experience of loss*. Washington, DC: American Psychological Association.

Neimeyer, R and Anderson, A (2002) Meaning reconstruction theory, in Thompson, N (ed) *Loss and grief*. Basingstoke: Palgrave.

Newburn, T (1993) *Disaster and after*. London: Jessica Kingsley.

Newman, T (2002) *Promoting resilience: A review of effective strategies for child care services*. Exeter: Centre for Evidence Based Social Services.

Oliver, M (1996) *Understanding disability*. Basingstoke: Palgrave.

Oliviere, D, Hargreaves, R and Monroe, B (eds) (1998) *Good practices in palliative care*. Aldershot: Ashgate.

Oswin, M (1990) The grief that does not speak. *Search*, Winter 45–7. (Also in Dickenson, D and Johnson, M (eds)(1993) *Death, dying and bereavement*. London: Sage).

Parinding, S and Achjadi, J (1988) *Toraja: Indonesia's mountain eden*. Singapore: Times Editions.

Parents against Child Sexual Abuse (1995) For mothers by mothers booklet. Leicestershire and Northamptonshire Social Services Departments.

Parkes, CM (1971) Psychosocial transitions: a field for study. *Social Science and Medicine*, 5: 101–15.

Parkes, CM (1996) *Bereavement (3rd edition)*. London: Routledge.

Parkes, CM (2006) *Love and loss*. London: Routledge.

Parkes, CM, Laungani, P and Young, B (eds) (1997) *Death and bereavement across cultures*. London: Routledge.

Parton, N (1996) *Social theory, social change and social work*. London: Routledge.

Payne, H (1990) *Creative movement and dance in groupwork*. Bicester: Winslow Press.

Payne, H (1993) *Handbook of inquiry in the arts therapies: One river, many currents*. London: Jessica Kingsley.

Payne, S, Horn, S and Relf, M (1999) *Loss and bereavement*. Buckingham: Open University Press.

Pennebaker, JW (1997) Writing about emotional experiences as a therapeutic process. *Psychological Science*, 8: 162–9.

Picardie, R (1998) *Before I say goodbye*. London: Penguin.

Prior, L (1989) *The social organisation of death, medical discourses and social practices in Belfast*. Basingstoke: Macmillan.

Quinn, A (1998) Learning from palliative care: concepts to underpin the transfer of knowledge from specialist palliative care to mainstream social work settings. *Social Work Education*, 17 (1): 9–19.

Rando, T (1988) *Grieving: How to go on living when someone you love dies*. Lexington, MA.: Lexington Books.

Rees, W (1971) The hallucinations of widowhood. *British Medical Journal*, 2 October, 4: 37–41.

Reoch, R (1997) *Dying well: a holistic guide for the dying and their carers*. London: Gaia.

Riches, G and Dawson, P (2000) *An intimate loneliness*. Buckingham: Open University Press.

Robinson, L (2007) *Cross-cultural child development for social workers*. Basingstoke: Palgrave.

Rose, R and Philpot, T (2005) *The child's own story: Life story work with traumatised children*. London: Jessica Kingsley.

Rosenblatt, P (1993) Cross cultural variation in the experience, expression and understanding of grief, in Irish, DP et al. (eds) *Ethnic variations in death, dying and grief: diversity in universality*. London: Taylor and Francis.

Rosenblatt, P (1997) Grief in small-scale societies, in Parkes, CM, Laungani, P and Young, B (eds) *Death and bereavement across cultures*. London: Routledge.

Sapey, B (2002) *Disability*, in Thompson, N (ed) *Loss and grief*. Basingstoke: Palgrave.

Seale, C (1998) *Constructing death: The sociology of dying and bereavement*. Cambridge: Cambridge University Press.

Sheldon, B (1986) Social work effectiveness experiments – review and implications. *British Journal of Social Work*,16 (2): 223–42.

Sheldon, F (1997) *Psychosocial palliative care*. Cheltenham: Stanley Thornes.

Shemmings, Y (1996) *Death, dying and residential care*. Aldershot: Avebury.

Small, N (2001) Theories of grief: a critical review, in Hockey, J, Katz, J and Small, N (eds) *Grief, mourning and death ritual*. Buckingham: Open University Press.

St. Christopher's Hospice (1998) *Candle: children, young people and loss*, Service Leaflet.

Steel, L and Kidd, W (2001) *The family*. Basingstoke: Palgrave.

Stroebe, M (1992) Coping with bereavement, a review of the grief. work hypothesis. *Omega*, 26: 19–42.

Stroebe, M (1997) From mourning and melancholia to bereavement and biography: an assessment of Walter's new model of grief. *Mortality*, 2 (3): 255–62.

Stroebe, M (1998) New directions in bereavement research: exploration of gender differences. *Palliative Medicine*, 12: 5–12.

Stroebe, M and Schut, H (1998) Culture and grief. *Bereavement Care*, 17 (1): 7–11.

Stroebe, M and Schut, H (1999) The dual process model of coping with bereavement: rationale and description. *Death Studies*, 23 (3): 197–224.

Stroebe, M and Schut, H (2001) Meaning making in the dual process model of coping with bereavement, in Neimeyer, R (ed) *Meaning reconstruction and the experience of loss*. Washington, DC: American Psychological Association.

Stroebe, MS, Hansson, RO, Stroebe, W and Schut, H (eds) (2001) *Handbook of bereavement research: Consequences, coping and care*. Washington, DC: APA.

Stroebe, M and Stroebe, W (1991) Does 'grief work' work? *Journal of Counselling and Clinical Psychology*, 59 (3): 479–82.

Stroebe, M, Schut, H and Stroebe, W (1998) Bereavement, in Friedman, H (ed) *Encyclopaedia of mental health*. San Diego, CA: Academic.

Stroebe, W, Stroebe, M, Abakoumin, G and Schut, H (1996) The role of loneliness and social support in adjustment to loss: A test of attachment versus stress theory. *Journal of Personality and Social Psychology*, 70 (6): 1241–9.

Stuart, S (1994) *Widowed young*. CRUSE Chronicle, October, 1–2.

Sudnow, D (1967) *Passing on: The social organisation of dying*. Englewood Cliffs, NJ: Prentice-Hall.

Sutcliffe, P, Tufnell, G and Cornish, U (1998) *Working with the dying and bereaved*. London: Macmillan.

Sweeting, H and Gilhooly, M (1997) Dementia and the phenomenon of social death. *Sociology of Health and Illness*, 19 (1): 93–117.

Thompson, A (1999) High anxiety. *Community Care*, 1–7 April, 18–19.

Thompson, N (2000) *Understanding social work*. Basingstoke: Palgrave.

Thompson, N (2001) *Anti-discriminatory practice (3rd edition)*. Basingstoke: Palgrave.

Thompson, N (2002a) Introduction. In Thompson, N (ed) *Loss and grief*. Basingstoke: Palgrave.

Thompson, N (ed) (2002b) *Loss and grief*. Basingstoke: Palgrave.

Thompson, S (2002) Older people, in Thompson, N (ed) *Loss and grief*. Basingstoke: Palgrave.

Thompson, S and Thompson, N (1999) Older people, crisis and loss. *Illness, Crisis and Loss*, 7 (2): 122–33.

Turner, V (1969) *The ritual process*. Harmondsworth: Penguin.

Upton, N (2001) Caregiver coping in dementing illness. Unpublished PhD Thesis, Anglia Polytechnic University.

Van Gennep, A (1960 [1909]) *The rites of passage*. London: Routledge and Kegan Paul.

Walter, T (1991) The mourning after Hillsborough. *The Sociological Review*, 39 (3): 599–625.

Walter, T (1994) *The revival of death*. London: Routledge.

Walter, T (1996) A new model of grief: Bereavement and biography. *Mortality*, 1 (1): 7–25.

Walter, T (1997) Letting go and keeping hold: A reply to Stroebe. *Mortality*, 2 (3): 263–6.

Warren, B (1993) *Using the creative arts in therapy: A Practical introduction*. London: Routledge.

Warren, J (2007) *Service user and carer participation in social work*. Exeter: Learning Matters.

Watson, S and Austerberry, H (1986) *Housing and homelessness – a feminist perspective*. London: Routledge.

Weinstein, J (2002) Teaching and learning about loss, in Thompson, N (ed) *Loss and grief*. Basingstoke: Palgrave.

Wikan, U (1988) Bereavement and loss in two Muslim communities: Egypt and Bali compared. *Social Science and Medicine*, 27 (5): 451–60.

Willmott, H (2000) Death. So what? Sociology, sequestration and emancipation. *The Sociological Review*, 48 (4): 649–665.

Worden, W (1991) *Grief counselling and grief therapy – a handbook for the mental health practitioner (2nd edition)*. London: Routledge (1st edition 1983 by Tavistock).

Worden, W (1996) *Children and grief*. London: Guilford Press.

Wortman, C and Silver, R (1989) The myths of coping with loss. *Journal of Consulting and Clinical Psychology*, 57: 349–57.

Yamamoto, T, Okonogi, K, Iwasaki, T and Yoshimura, S. (1969) Mourning in Japan. *American Journal of Psychiatry*, 125, 1660–5.

Index